THE NINE DOORS OF MIDGARD

THE NINE DOORS OF MIDGARD

A Curriculum of Rune-Work

Third Revised and Expanded Edition

EDRED

Yrmin-Drighten of the Rune-Gild

2003

ISBN: 1-885972-23-7

Published by
RÛNA-RAVEN PRESS
P.O. Box 557
Smithville, Texas 78957

Printed in the United States of America

This Book is Dedicated to
the Rune-Gilders

VI

Acknowledgments

I would like to take this opportunity to acknowledge the help and support given to me over the years of the development of the Rune-Gild by Crystal Dawn; Mitchell Edwin Wade, Drighten; Robert Zoller, Rune-Master; Ian Read, Rune-Master; Dr. Michael Aquino, Drighten; James A. Chisholm, Rune-Master; Alice Rhoades, Rune-Master; David Bragwin James, and Ralph Tegtmeier. Thanks also go to Timothy Weinmeister, Fellow, for the original cover art, to Dianne Ross, Fellow, for her help in preparing the original manuscript of this work, and to John Wilson for his corrections for this third edition.

Table of Contents

VIII

X

Preface to the Third Edition

This is already a thrice-born book. Its embryonic beginning was as a series of privately printed exercises, over time expanded into a book-length work for exclusive use within the Rune-Gild. This was essentially published commercially by Llewellyn in 1991 as a trade paperback. When general support for the book was withdrawn by the publisher it went out of print for a time until it was reprinted in a utilitarian edition by Rûna-Raven in 1997. It is now being reissued in a revised and expanded form, once more as a trade paperback.

This is a book of self-transformation and so it is fitting that the book itself would go through many metamorphoses— each time growing in substance, surviving against the odds, yet always evolving toward that mystery which it already *is*. This edition is a new life for an old book.

The *Nine Doors* form a universal paradigm of exercises which has been used to excellent effect by individuals working outside the Germanic esoteric idiom. For example, it has been adapted to the idioms of the Celtic *ogham* and the Greek CTOIXEIA. *The Nine Doors of Midgard* is the part of the inner Rune-Gild which faces outward toward the world. It demonstrates just the superficial level of the teachings of the Gild— and those who practice its exercises from, *de facto*, a function of the Gild. The *Nine Doors* are the *gift* of the Gild to the world. (A special Gild-only edition of the *Nine Doors* is scheduled to appear in 2005.)

The Rune-Gild itself is an entirely *traditional* school of self-development almost entirely dependent upon subtle transmissions of individualized inFormation from teacher to pupil, from master to Learner or Fellow. The exercises and curriculum contained in these pages — or their equivalent — are a basic prerequisite for advancement in the traditional school. Information on the Gild is printed as Appendix C. The fundamental work of the *Nine Doors* is that of 1) internalizing the runestaves as an inner reality and mentally cross-fertilizing that newly installed symbolic pattern with mythic information drawn from a curriculum of readings in primary and secondary sources.

Work with the *Nine Doors* cannot turn a mustard seed into an oak tree, yet it can feed and water the acorn that might have otherwise withered, until it indeed becomes that mighty oak.

Edred
Woodharrow
September 20, 2003

Preface to the Second Edition

As a working experiment the text of *The Nine Doors of Midgard* was printed commercially in 1991 by Llewellyn Publications. The purpose of the experiment was to see if making the basic curriculum of the Gild widely available would increase interest in the Gild and *esoterica Germanica* in general. The effect was one of making the world aware of just how serious and profound our traditions and training methods are. The effect on the membership of the Gild itself was quite small. Early In 1997 we learned that Llewellyn would discontinue publication of the book due to poor sales. Reviewers were pretty unanimous in their opinion that this manual was only for those totally dedicated to the Germanic path of development— and *total dedication* to anything is hard to come by in the world of occultizoid nincompoops.

The Nine Doors of Midgard is not meant for denizens of that world. This training manual is for a new breed of individuals who understand the meaning of the timeless teaching embodied in the Watch-Word of the Gild: *Reyn til Rúna!* Those who understand this will follow a three-fold method of development: 1) objective study, 2) subjective synthesis and 3) total activization. The curriculum of the Nine Doors is especially valuable as a tool for working on the second part of this formula.

This book is not designed to be available in bookstores. It is mainly intended for those Working within the Rune-Gild, or for those who plan to enter the Rune-Gild at some time in their careers.

Indeed, if one follows the curriculum outlined in this book results will be evident. But to follow it faithfully one must be willing to dedicate at least a year or two to the exclusive pursuit of the symbolism and lore outlined here. This book is not intended to be used as just a part of a jumble of alternative ideas. The lore of the Runes forms a coherent and profound *whole*. To pursue the path exclusively is to pursue it intensely.

For members of the Rune-Gild this text is to be used in conjunction with that of the *Gildisbók*, the inner guide to the Rune-Gild program.

The preface to the first edition has here been revised to reflect the current policies and teachings of the Rune-Gild.

Edred
Woodharrow
August 20, 1997ce

XIII

Revised Preface to the First Edition

The Nine Doors of Midgard is the magical curriculum of the Rune-Gild. This preface is intended to set record straight on the nature and aims of the Rune-Gild, the character of the work upon which the Runer is about to embark and the shape and wise of the roads upon which the Runer will travel.

The lore of the Rune-Gild is based on and *is* essentially that of the most traditional from of Runelore. The basis of our work is not in any essential way dependent on the *revelation* of any living Runemaster. What is essential about our work can actually be summed up in a very few words and signs— the rest is, or can be, left up to the individual. However, history has shown us that this is not as easy as it might at first appear. The vast majority of Runers need help of some kind at various times in their runic careers. For most this comes at the very beginning of their exposure to the *mysteries*. It is one of the main tasks of the Rune-Gild to provide that help at this stage.

The basic teaching of the Gild is traditional. We shun the spurious runic systems that have been spawned in recent years by persons totally outside the Odian stream of consciousness. After the basic tradition has been learned on inner levels, the Runer will be encouraged to explore and innovate *in the true spirit of the Runes* and of their High Drighten, Wōden. However, it can not be too strongly emphasized that the Learner or Fellow who might come up with a radically new approach to something, or something that seems to run counter to the tradition as known by the Gild, is urged to consult with a Rune-Master on the matter. He or she would certainly be warned against assuming that his or her *subjective* realization is of *universal* value. It is much more likely that it is of personal, and even temporary value. Too often the half-learned jump to the conclusion that if something is true for them it must be true for the next person. That is how we end up with subjectively created systems and books with no basis in the tradition. Only a Master of the Gild can determine what is universally valid for the tradition, and such determinations are made only with the greatest deliberation on many levels.

The structure of the Rune-Gild is one which provides the basics in a traditional manner and leaves the details up to the individual. The over-all structuring of your work comes more and more under the control of the Runer as he or she rises in the Gild. In the beginning, however, you are encouraged to follow the program of work fairly closely. (This is especially true for those who have not undertaken a regular "occult" training program before.) But even having said this, I must hasten to add that in minor details of daily working activities the Runer is absolutely free to do what he or she feels is significant or appropriate.

You should begin to exercise your inventiveness early, but in small ways. For example, the High Rede might get a letter from a new Runer who anxiously asks: "What color should the hilt of my knife be?" The tradition has nothing specific to say on this count. The Runer is free— is obligated to take some spiritual initiative and consciously decide on a color that is significant for him or her. The Odian is traditional, but one of the mainstays of our tradition is independence and innovation. These factors must be balanced. The Gild is not out to manufacture "psychic slaves" who will be told what to do at every moment they are working. This would be anti-Odian.

To some extent the Gild is a network of outsiders— lone wolves who recognize in each other the same essence and most importantly the same *heritage*.

Our tradition is based on the 24 Runes of the Elder Fuþark, the Rune names, and the Rune poems. Our lore is informed by the highest type of intellectual and magical learning. The Odian shuns neither the intellect nor intuition, but seeks to have these faculties work in harmony within the tradition. This is our birthright.

When all is said and done, there are as many roads to the Runes as there are Odians traveling them. No two Runers are exactly alike, and thus their pathways to the Runes will inevitably be different in many regards. This is what we expect. Just as no two people speak *exactly* the same language (each of us carries a unique grammar of our own language within us), we can still make ourselves understood— but only because we share similar structures and experiences with those who belong to our linguistic group. The implications of this are obvious for the Gild. We must learn the basic, traditional symbolic language of the Runes — that secret language originally given to us by the God Wōden — but we must at the same time expect that we will *speak* a form of it hat is slightly different from anyone else's.

The overall character of the work of the Gild falls into three main categories: 1) self-work, 2) lore-work, and 3) Gild-work. The first is the main subject of the Nine Doors of Midgard— the work of self-transformation. This is supplemented by lore-work, which is basically the intellectual learning and understanding of Runelore. Runelore is the traditional esoteric Germanic philosophy and cosmology. This second line feeds the first and together they provide the *common language* with which you can communicate with your fellows. Complementary to Runelore is Gild-work, which is the Runers' contribution to the Gild— in the form of work (writings or organizational work), tolls, and galdor (magical work). This latter category can only be engaged in by those who are formally affiliated with the Gild, of course. All three of these streams must be developed more or less simultaneously and in harmony. One can not be practiced to the exclusion of the others. All lead ultimately to deep level transformation of the self and of the world— which is the ultimate goal of the Gild and each of its Runers.

Now the time has come to lay out in more detail what the exact nature of the Odian is. Actually this question can only be answered through one's own realization in the final analysis. However, again there are certain traits or characteristics that are common enough. Many Runers might even find some of what is said here shocking or strange. To those I can only say: "What did you expect?" When one becomes involved in *mysteries* one should expect the unexpected; when one seeks out *secrets* one should expect that they will often be difficult to uncover and to grasp.

First of all, concerning the term *Odian*: This indicates, as opposed to the term *Odinist*, one who does not *worship* the God Óðinn (Wōden), but rather emulates him. The Odinist worships, the Odian becomes himSelf. This is the true nature of the cult of Óðinn. The Odian does not seek union with Óðinn, but rather with his own unique self. This is the godly task of Óðinn himself. If we were to seek to abdicate our selfhoods to any force, Óðinn would only look on in disgust. True Odians are few and far between.

What are then the essential characteristics of the work of the Odian? This can be summed up in four adjectives. The Odian is: bi-polar, egoistic, transformative, and cooperative. Each of these characteristics deserve full discussion.

Bipolarity indicates that the Odian stands in the middle between two extremes, between fire and ice, between Asgard and Hel, and that he shuns neither but clearly recognizes the necessity of both and seeks the experience of both— of light and dark. The Odian is bi-polar in that he seeks darkness as well as light, he seeks in the branches of Yggdrasill as well as among its roots. One of the greatest secrets of Rune-Odianism is its bi-polar path. It is in stark contrast to most systems which simply aim in one direction, and reject the opposite. This would lead to an atmosphere of *good* and *evil*, of a moral dualism which is totally foreign to the Odian path. The Odian can be truly beyond good and evil. He can get beyond these terms by identifying all polar extremes, seeking them, experiencing them, and thereby recognizing that it is only in his own Self that these poles have meaning. Only by realizing the highest and the lowest is the true middle found, only in the twilight between darkness and light does the true self shine.

It is the brightness of this individual self that the Odian seeks to develop. In following the Odian path the Runer goes his *own* way. This is a way that honors individual differences and seeks to enhance the quality of that uniqueness rather than see them swallowed up in a mass mind. This is precisely why it is we who are the *true*, if hidden, guardians of the *folk* and not those who merely seek to be subsumed in an organic whole. The All-Father demands of his chosen that they each shine with a unique light recognizable as an individual ego or *ek*.

However, this *ek* (the old Germanic form of the word *I*) is not merely the unexamined, untested, natural ego which non-Runers usually must simply accept or fight. This is a self-concept shaped and nurtured by the will in accordance with the principles of the Odian path. So this is the result of a transformative process in which raw self-stuff is re-shaped into an image designed by the conscious will illuminated and informed by the gods and ancestral memory. The path of the Odian is one of unending change which knows that a new stage of being always lies hidden just beyond the horizon. It is this knowledge which leads us to our restless power of continuous transformation and constant innovation. Contrary to the image projected by most of the Odinist and Ásatrú movement, ours (i.e. the Odian) should not be a backward looking or anachronistic path, but rather one which is in its very essence innovative and transformative.

Finally, Odianism is a force which must work together with various groups of an Ásatrú/Odinist kind, as well as other groups with which the All-Father has made contact in recent years. It is the heritage of the Odian to ensure the continued and vigorous development and health of the folk and of the host society at large. Odianism co-operates with them but will always outside the mainstream, we will always be outsiders— so it was in days of yore, and so shall it ever be. But we were then, and are now, dedicated to the well-being of the whole. This service is our eternal duty right along with our duty to ourselves to gather in power and forever shape and re-shape whatever we find to be in accordance with our enlightened ends.

You are now embarking on practical work with the Runes. Many Runers will have already done some type of inner work before, while for others this will be the first time. This is the most important work a person can do, of course, and it requires a proper attitude and will in order to be successful. The main virtues in this endeavor are: action, self-reliance, perseverance, and self-forgiveness. First, *do*— begin the work at once. Do not wait for "the perfect time," or say to yourself: "I'm not quite ready yet..." Second, learn to follow your instincts and be reliant on yourself to answer questions of small details in your work. What is most important is that you learn the mainstays of your work. Once this is done, all else should almost follow of its own accord. Third, stick to it. This program is designed as if the Runer were to work *every day*. This is ideal and you should aim for at least five days a week (especially for *Doors* 1 - 4) but we know that this can not always be done. Which brings us to self-forgiveness. When you are unable to work— do not throw up your hands in disgust. Know that those things will happen, these moods will come and go, and as long as you persevere you can forgive yourself these shortcomings— for no one else can or will. Sometimes it is even preferable and beneficial to lay off work for periods in order to assimilate your results.

XVII

The Rune-Gild program is a means to certain ends. But the ends are the important things: knowledge, power, wisdom, self-transformation, and service to folk.

Edred, Yrmin-Drighten
June 21, 1997ev

Introduction

This work is the first systematic introduction to Runelore available in many centuries. This age requires and allows some new approaches to be sure. We have changed over the centuries in question. But at the same time we are as traditional as possible. The Gild does not fear innovation — in fact we embrace it — but only after the tradition has been thoroughly examined for all it has to offer. Too often in the history of the runic revival various proponents have actually taken their preconceived notions about what the Runes should say— and then "runicized" them. We avoid this type of pseudo-innovation at all costs.

Our over-all magical method is a simple one. The tradition posits an outer-world (objective reality) and an inner-world (subjective reality). The work of the Runer is the exploration of both of these worlds for what they have to offer in the search for wisdom. In learning the Runes, the Runer synthesizes all the objective lore and tradition he can find on the Runes with his subjective experience. In this way he "makes the Runes his own." All the Runes and their overall system are then used as a sort of "meta-language" in meaningful communication between these objective and subjective realities. The Runer may wish to be active in this communication — to cause changes to occur in accordance with his will, or he may wish to learn from one of these realities some information which would normally be hidden from him. This is magic and divination respectively. Never is the Runer totally passive, because despite the existence of these two realities, the Runic fact is that the Runer lives in a third state (at least when he is fully aware) in the Self — which is capable of observing what is generally called both the subjective and objective universes from an *omni*jective viewpoint.

Most simply put, the work of the Nine Doors is that learning of the Runes and using them in self-directed and conscious work in a traditional framework which can be evaluated by the Gild-Masters.

General Introduction to the Rune-Gild
and the Curriculum of the Nine Doors

The Rune Gild

The Rune-Gild has grown and evolved internally since its ceremonial foundation in 1980ev — and through this time it has become ever more fitted to its aims which are 1) the guidance, information, and recognition (=initiation) of suitable Gilders (members of the Rune-Gild itself), 2) the rediscovery, redevelopment and evolution of the entire spectrum of Germanic esoteric sciences (=Runelore), and 3) the welding of these great aims into an institution dedicated to the continuing development of the Odian Way in the world. The Rune-Gild is a completely independent institution with no official ties to any Neo-Germanic religious organization, or any other religious organization for that matter. However, its secondary goal is the nourishment of all institutions that seek the glory of the Great God of the Gild, the Lord of Light and the Drighten of Darkness— Wōden.

As one on the threshold of entering the Gild, these first few pages are intended to inform you concerning the basic goals, organizational principles, initiatory system, and magical work of the Rune-Gild.

Goals of the Gild

One of the deep underlying goals of Gild-work is the establishment and maintenance of a true numinous magical link with the God of the Gild, Wōden. This link will benefit the evolution of individuals within the Gild, the Gild itself, as well as other institutions with links with the Odian stream or current. The way in which individual Gilders are brought into contact with the full power of this stream is through the initiatory system of the Gild— the Nine Doors of Midgard. As one works through the Nine Doors, one will soon learn that this is not a structure of dogma or of programming to a standard belief system, but rather a pathway to *individual* evolution within a well established tradition. The Gild is not for "believers," but for seekers, who are always on the vanguard of new beginnings. The Nine Doors may seem to be extensive and complete— but they are really only tiny openings cast once again in a traditional form for the first time in more than a millennium. But it is the work of all Runers to forge their own roadways through these Doors.

The initiatory paths of the Gilder will provide the experience necessary to the development of those individuals needed to watch over and guide the evolution of the other Gilders and of the Gild structure as a whole.

Gilders will have as their goals the evolution of Self, the conversion of that development into communicable forms, and the sharing of those forms with their fellow Gilders. In this we follow the Way of Wōden. This research will take many forms, as determined by the individuals involved; however, it is the hope of the High Rede that a range of work on the outer forms as well as inner processes of Odianism will emerge from the Gild as a whole.

The results of this hidden work will be put into communicable forms — printed matter, audio- and/or video-tapes — and distributed privately to the proper Gilders within the Gild and often commercially to the general public.

Organization of the Gild
and its System of Initiation

The Rune-Gild is made up of Gilders (members) at three levels of initiation: I. Learners (apprentices), II. Fellows (journeymen), and III. Rune-Masters (masters). All those who are accepted into the Gild are brought in at the level of Learner. They can then begin the work of the Nine Doors of Midgard within the Gild under the guidance of the contents of the *Gildisbók*, of their personal mentor (a Gild-Master assigned by the Gild), as well as participate in Outer Hall Workings with fellow Gilders. The work of the Nine Doors may take up to four years to complete. Many individuals who have done considerable work of this kind already will, however, progress much faster. Still others may take somewhat longer. After the Learners have worked with the system and with the tradition under the guidance of their mentors certain special areas of interest and/or talent will begin to emerge. As these do, the Learner is expected to put his or her findings and experiences into a communicable form most suitable to the type of work being done. It may be expository prose, poetry, music, sculpture, ritual, or any number of things. All Gilders will have their own personal mixture of these modes of expression. In the Ninth Door you can read extensive instructions on how to create your "Master Piece." After you have demonstrated your basic knowledge of the exoteric and esoteric principles of the runic tradition — including a *summary* and analysis of your Nine Doors of Midgard work — you will be eligible to be Named, or initiated as a Fellow in the Rune-Gild. Such Namings are done by the Gild-Masters— usually in person at one of the Gild-Moots. The main things for the Learner to keep in mind are: 1) *to work* and after reaping the harvest of that work, 2) *to communicate* those results to the High Rede in two forms a) a general summary and analysis of the Nine Doors work, and b) some general *application* of your skills.

After the Learner is Named a Fellow and is ceremonially installed in that office, he or she begins a period of more extensive personal interaction with the Rune-Masters. The Fellow is to undertake some specialized important work within the tradition of the Gild— again this is not necessarily a purely *intellectual* matter. He or she becomes a true journey-man of the soul. The special project will end in a "masterpiece" that again may be executed in a variety of media. It will be judged by the High Rede, and if found worthy of a master, the Fellow will be eligible to be Named and installed as a Rune-Master in the Gild.

The chief responsibilities of the Rune-Masters are: 1) to ensure the continued esoteric growth of themselves and of the aims of the Gild, 2) to aid Learners and Fellows in their work, and 3) to help administer the Gild as called upon by the High Rede and the Yrmin-Drighten.

In a simple scheme then, the structure of and work of the Gild can be summarized:

The Rune-Gild	
Level	Work/Duties
I. Learner (apprentice)	1) Nine Doors of Midgard curriculum (+ report) 2) General free application of the principles of the Nine Doors in objective form.
II. Fellow (journeyman)	Specialized project (Masterpiece)
III. Rune-Master (master)	1) Continued self-growth 2) Leadership of Learners and Fellows 3) Administration

In the final analysis, the whole is arranged much as a university (or as a university should be) in that the apprentice follows a core curriculum of basics (= undergraduate) the Fellow pursues a self-generated project of specialized work (=graduate), and the Rune-Master is the ultimate product of the system: the magister or doctor.

All Rune-Masters of the Gild are equals among themselves in matters of inner work— the tasks taken up by individual Rune-Masters will probably be so unique that they will certainly have to find their own inner guide from within (and much of the work of the Nine Doors is directed to this final end). For purposes of administering the Gild on an ongoing basis, the High Rede (made up of no more than nine Rune-Masters) will oversee the development and maintenance of the whole body. These Rune-Masters will be elected or Named by the Yrmin-Drighten— who himself was called forth by both Wōden and wyrd.

For a more general introductory view of the Gild, see Appendix C in which the introductory material sent out to those who make direct inquiries to the Gild is printed.

Nature of Initiation in the Gild

True initiation consists of two aspects 1) the recognition of the candidates attainment of a certain level of being, and 2) the in-Formation of the candidate in the tradition. The first recognizes a fact, the second propels the candidate toward the next level of achievement. In the Learner-initiation, one is recognized as a Learner in the Gild, and set on the path toward becoming a Fellow. In the in-Formation aspects the Gilder is placed in a certain frame of reference through inner work, learning, and thinking so that certain innate characteristics may develop within the self— each in its own way. Neither the Gild nor any Rune-Master has the power to convey to you — all Odian power must be born from within the self. We *can* lead you to the right steads, at the right tides, for Odian becoming to unfold within you in the age-old ways— and as fellows within the ring we can name you as one among us.

There is a guide and a force that will lead and pull, give vision and power — but it is in-dwelling and belongs to you alone. Along the roadways of Yggdrasill you will come to know this entity, and he or she will show you the way to lift you up into your god-self— which is the ultimate task of all Rune-Masters. This entity is the only true *initiator*.

The Structure of the Doors

Each Door or section of this curriculum will be introduced by an *Opening* segment which will orient you in the current Door. It will tell you what intellectual information you should be assimilating during the time period encompassed by the Door. This will mainly come in the form of books from the bibliography in this book.

The Opening will also contain a general discussion of the plan of daily work, especially if it differs in any great way from previous Doors.

The body of each Door is divided into sections discussing the various exercises or kinds of work to be undertaken during the progress of that Door. Most of these will be in several parts developed over the course of a series of Doors.

Working habits developed in the First Door should be continued throughout all subsequent Doors.

RÛNA

and the Work of the Gild

The entire contents and mechanics of the Nine Doors of Midgard program should be understood as one way to approach the charge of the Rune-Gild: *Reyn til Rúna!* This is an Old Norse or Icelandic phrase meaning "Seek toward the Mysteries!" *Rúna* is the eternal Mystery or Secret — absolute and dynamic — from which the "individual" Runes are derived The program of the Nine Doors offers a day-by-day plan for those embarking on this journey— a plan which will result in many Runes being revealed to the Runer. A Runer is one who *actively* engages him or herself in the quest for the Mystery through the path of the Runes.

There is a great and overarching methodology to this quest, which has been perhaps so far been best explained in the *Gildisbók*. In essence this method is one of first gathering and studying in an objective manner all that can be *known* of a tradition, then setting about to absorb subjectively the contents of that tradition and finally to enact that subjective (inner) synthesis. This final step sheds new light on the results of the first, and further deepens the results of the second leading to more potent action once more in the third phase. This cycle of **knowledge-insight-action** is an unending one. This Nine Doors program is conceived of as a tool to be especially helpful in the second part of this process.

The Watch-Word: *Rúna* is the guide to all that the Gild is and seeks to become. Under its guidance the whole of the world is being reconfigured once more. *Rúna* is the great Unknown and Unknowable which pulls the mind of Man and God ever onward and upward to greater Knowledge and Power. It is this *Rúna* which Óðinn confronts and assimilates in the Yggdrasill-initiation, after which he synthesizes and expresses for the first time the ordered and articulated **fuþark**. Reenacting this process in an inner way is the essence of the Nine Doors Work, and is a central method in the actualization of *Rúna* in the lives of individuals.

Reyn til Rúna!

The First Door of Midgard
— Opening —

Before you embark through the First Door of Midgard, you should be familiar with the material in *Runelore* by Edred and with the contents of at least one of the basic introductions to Germanic religion and mythology listed in the bibliography. You should also decide whether you wish to become formally affiliated with the Gild, or whether you will just be using the Gild curriculum as a part of your own private work. If you chose to affiliate with the Gild, you will be sent a document outlining the rites and oaths to be taken. Otherwise just continue with the work of the Nine Doors as outlined here. You can chose to join the Gild at any time in the future, and you will be welcome.

Begin your Gild-work on a day which is significant to you. This schedule represents the work to be done on a daily basis and its ordering within a daily working session:

1) Hammer Hallowing (see Door II)
2) Daily Rite of Dedication
3) Vocalic Breathing
4) Concentration-visualization Exercise
5) *Staða* Exercise
6) Closing Formula
and 7) PAD Work

If your PAD work (see below) is done in a formal meditative way, include it in your session between the *staða* exercise and the closing formula.

You may wish to perform the work more than once a day, or you may want to some single exercise more often — all that is up to each individual Runer. It may or may not hasten your progress.

Choose a regular time and place to cultivate the habit of daily going to your private *vé* (sacred enclosure) and doing your holy duty to your forebears and to your gods and goddesses.

The program of daily work outlined here should not last over 30 minutes at its longest stage of development.

Make a special notebook, called the *Galdor-Book* (GB), in which you will rewrite all exercises, rituals, etc., in your own hand and record all your work, results, and progress on a day to day basis. Let this *Galdor-Book* be the book from which you work each day. Evaluate your performance on each part of the program every day— with suggestions to yourself on how you could improve. You might also want to record other events of magical significance to you in the Galdor-Book.

Reading

The Runer should begin a reading program of works drawn from the bibliography printed at the end of this book. At the beginning of every Door there will be suggestions as to what works would be most helpful during the period covered by that Door's work. However, the Runer is really encouraged to go beyond the list and incorporate other comparable works into the reading program. Works that appear with an asterisk are **required**, and have contents so unique that they can not be replaced by other titles.

Suggested reading for the First Door:

Runelore, Edred
Futhark, Edred
Rune-Song, Edred
*"How to Be a Heathen" in *Blue Rûna*, Stephen E. Flowers
"The Idea of Integral Culture" S. E. Flowers
Rune-Might, Edred
Runes, Ralph Elliott
Introduction to English Runes, R.I. Page
Runes, R.I. Page
*The Art and Practice of Getting Material Things Through
    Creative Visualization*, Ophiel.
Concentration, Mouni Sadu
Seeing with the Mind's Eye, Mike and Nancy Samuels.
Concentration, Ernest Wood

WORKINGS

To begin the training program of the Nine Doors of Midgard, the Runer should start on a day of some significance (personal or traditional) to the idea of new beginnings. The nights just before a full moon, or just after a new moon are ideal. For those outside the Rune-Gild the simple inner affirmation that you will begin the program and remain true to its process is quite enough. This is then coupled with the daily Rite of Dedication to be used by all Runers in the Nine Doors program. For those formally affiliated with the Gild, there is a Lone Rite of Entry to be performed. Rites of daily work are to be performed as opening and closing ceremonies for the formalized sessions of exercises— but certainly need not be carried out each time you wish to practice an exercise in an odd free moment, or in connection with less formal exercises.

Before beginning the daily exercise program, perform the following:

Daily Rite of Dedication
(Daily Work of Self-Giving)

1) Stand erect and face north. Recite "Hávamál" 138-139 in English or
the original Old Norse:

I know that I hung   on a windy tree,
     nights all-nine,
wounded by the gar   given to Óðinn,
     myself to myself,
on that tree,   of which no man knoweth
     from what roots it rises.

They dealt me no bread   nor drinking horn,
     I looked down;
I took up the Runes   roaring I took them,
     and fell back again.

----
or

Veit ek at ek hekk   vindgameiði á
     nætr allar níu
geiri undaðr   ok gefinn Óðni,
     sjálfr sjálfum mér
á þeim meiði,   er mangi veit
     hvers hann af rótum renn.
Við hleifi mik sældu   né við hornigi
     nysta ek niðr;
nam ek upp rúnar   œpandi nam
     fell ek aptr þaðan.

2) Then with your arms stretched out at 45 degree angles overhead (Y-
staða), recite:

This holy day,   from dawn to dusk,
     myself to myself I give
     and from dusk to dawn anew,
     Hroptr has my mind all-whole.
I give myself to the wondrous Rune-work— in this hour and
throughout the day— I shall work my will!

3) Place your right hand on the gand and sax on your harrow before
you and say:
By gand and sax, ever shall I stay true to the oaths of the Gild!
(This is only for members of the Rune-Gild.)

4) Then say: **So shall it be!**

At the end of the formal daily exercise session, perform the following:
Closing Formula
(End Work)
1) Stand erect, facing north. Place arms at a 90o angle straight out from the body (cross-position) and recite "Hávamál" 164 (in English or Old Norse):

Now are Hárr's sayings said,   in Hárr's hall,
       helpful to the sons of men,
       but of no help to etins' sons;
hail, the one who speaks them   hail the one who knows them!
       gain, the one who gets them,
       hail, those who hear them!

----

or

Nú eru Háva mál kveðin   Háva höllu í,
       allþorf ýta sonum,
       óþorf jötna sonum;
heill, sá er kvað,   heill, sá er kann!
       njóti, sá er nam,
       heilir, þeirs hlyddu!

2) Turn to all four quarters — or to the airts if you are already used to working with them — and draw your arms in touching your solar plexus with your finger tips, balancing all forces raised in the exercises and rites in your personal center.

Personal Analysis Diary I
(Life-Work)

This is the first step in a program of self analysis in which you carefully consider all of your personal strengths and weaknesses and record them. The purpose of this program is the ultimate strengthening of your good points, which are boons to your life's aims, and the eventual elimination or neutralization of all personal weaknesses as a step toward the *willed* re-shaping of your personality in accordance with an *inspired* vision of your whole being.

Make a special notebook, called the Personal Analysis Diary, or Life-Book, which may be incorporated into the Galdor-Book, or be kept as a separate book. Begin by meditating upon "who" and "where" you are, and "who" and "where" you want to be— both in the short term (next month, next year) and long term (in 10, 20, or 30 years). In short, determine your present state of being — and willfully form an idea of the ways in which you must alter that state. Write all your introspections in your notebook in an orderly fashion.

These meditations may simply take the form of casual introspection (which you may conduct at odd times in the day set aside for this purpose), or you may supplement this more-or-less constant introspection with a ritualized form of meditation in which you sing the names Wōðanaz-Wiljōn-Wīhaz (or some variation of those names) for a period of one to two minutes, then lapse into a deep level of introspection. This charges your *hugr* (hugh) — the intellect or mind — with the qualities of this triad of gods. Actually they are all hypostases of the god generally known as Óðinn (Wōden). Their names mean "Master of Inspiration," "Strong Will," and "Holiness" respectively. These beginning meditations/introspections should continue for at least two weeks — but not much more than that — then go on to the next phase...

You begin the second phase of the PAD process by simultaneously forming two lists of qualities, habits, personal/personality characteristics, conditions, etc. The first list, the *bright* list, is to be made up of those things advantageous to your willed direction and which you generally consider to be your strengths. The second list, the *murk* list, is to be made up of those things disadvantageous to your willed direction and which you consider to be weaknesses. *Be absolutely brutal with yourself!* Your ability to re-shape your life harmoniously, and in accordance with your will is dependent upon an honest and true self-evaluation.

This listing process should go on for at least three weeks — but not more than five at the initial stage. Again you may use a formal meditational or informal introspective approach — or a combination of both. The PAD is to be kept absolutely private. The Gild Hall does not want copies of these lists. Reports on the progress you have made as a result of using the process would, of course, be of interest once success has been achieved.

Vocalic Breathing I

The discipline of vocalic breathing is one fundamental to the right working of Rune-songs or galdor (magical incantations, *mantras*, etc.), which will be developed in future steps of the Gild-Work. This practice has been most recently outlined in a runic context by the German magician, Karl Spiesberger, in his book *Runenexerzietien für Jedermann*.

Assume a posture (*staða*) which promotes both relaxation and attentive concentration. This may be either sitting, standing, or even lying down on your back. Begin the exercise by setting up a cycle of regular breathing — one with which you feel comfortable. You may let personal experience and experimentation guide you to some extent. But keep in mind that a *full* cycle of breath consists of four parts: 1) inhalation, 2 holding (in), 3) exhalation, and 4) holding (out). Also, be sure that your lungs are completely filled and emptied on each cycle. This must be done by filling your lungs from the bottom to top by first pushing the diaphragm down, then filling the body of the lungs, and finally by lifting the shoulders to fill the tops of the lungs. Reverse this process from top to bottom upon exhalation. These instructions on breath should also be followed in the *staða* exercises.

For vocalic breathing, in preparation for galdor-work, an unbalanced breath-rhythm is favored; for example, 5 seconds inhalation, 3 seconds hold, 7 seconds exhalation, 3 seconds hold. This is , of course, because the actively projected Rune-songs will be articulated on the exhalation. For the sake of full experimentation, however, the Runer is encouraged to work with a balanced inhalation/exhalation ratio as well.

Once this rhythm has been established (with 10-15 complete cycles), begin the vocalic breath. This may be done by "vibrating" one of the five main vowel sounds (exclusive of the runic ♪). To vibrate a sound you must sonorously articulate it from your diaphragm — from the center of your being — from where it vibrates throughout your entire system, while you fully concentrate on the process. This can also be done in silence, as an internal vibration. The sound vibrates from the center of your being and reverberates back from the limits of the world. With each breath cycle sing another vowel sound until you have completed all five. Then begin the vowel cycle again. Two orderings for the sounds will be found to be most useful in the beginning: 1) A.U.E.I.O, and 2) U.A.I.E.O. The reasons for these orderings will become clearer in the later Doors. Note that the latter ordering is that in which the vowels actually come in the fuþark row. Remember to keep your rhythmic breath under close control.

Also, you must keep your vowel qualities clear and *pure*. Many English speakers especially tend to "glide" their vowels into diphthongs. You may prevent this by ensuring that your jaw does not change position during articulation. The vowel qualities for this work are as follows:

a	[ah]	as the "a" in *father*
u	[oo]	as the "u" in *rule*
i	[ee]	as the "ee" in *greet*
e	[a]	as the "a" in *gate*
o	[o]	as the "o" in *go*

Concentrate upon the *sound* of the vowel throughout the cycle of breath. Concentrate upon it silently as you inhale and hold, mentally meld your consciousness with the sound as it enters your being, then project it — physically vibrating the sound — while intensively concentrating on the tone. On the last phase of the cycle, silently hear the echo of the sound reverberating off the distant angles of space. During each cycle, consciously identify yourself with the sound and with the physical apparatus which produced it.

Begin doing this exercise for about two minutes, and add 30 seconds each day (holding at plateaus for a couple of days if you feel the need to solidify your concentration), until you can comfortably do this work with a deep level of attention for about ten minutes.

Concentration-Visualization I

Under this heading fall a number of exercises of a general nature, as well as of a traditional runic kind. You can experiment with the mental exercises 1-3 as you will — they can provide many openings. But the Rune-Thinking must be worked as outlined every day.

Mental Exercises

The following exercises are intended to help develop the will necessary to the Rune-work. The concentration visualization exercises should all be performed with a naturally comfortable, but regular breath rhythm.

1) Gather a few (6-9) small, simple everyday objects of various shapes and colors, the black cloth (see below), and a neutral background surface. Sit in a comfortable, relaxed position with these things before you within easy reach and 2-3 feet from your eyes. Also, before you, back some distance, there should be a single natural light source, such as a candle. Place three of the objects on the neutral surface and cover them with the cloth. Relax and mentally close out any distractions. Now, shift the objects around beneath the cloth. Remove the cloth and study the things for three to four minutes. Without touching them, fix their colors, textures, shapes, shadows, relationships to each other, sizes — in short every factor you can — in your mind's eye. Now, again cover the objects with the cloth. Close your eyes and progressively build up in your imagination a picture of what you have been looking at. Do this in complete detail, full color, and in three dimensions. Do not lose heart if it is not complete at first— this is hard work. Work on the image at least as long as you looked at it, and then lift the cloth. Hold the image you had built up in your mind and compare it to what you see before you. Again study the objects, and again lower the cloth. Close your eyes and correct any errors in your vision. Use every device you can to build and detail the objects. Repeat the actual observation and image-building several times until you feel at ease with the result. But do not exceed a total period of 30 minutes. As your ability grows, add more items to the group, one item at a time. Vary the arrangement each time, and occasionally vary the objects.

2) before proceeding to exercise 3, this stage must be satisfactorily

completed. Thought watching is just that— a careful, concentrated, and energetic observation of thought with no attempt to control it. For the first few days, just allow your thoughts to wander freely and observe *how* your particular psychophysical complex reacts to being allowed this freedom, and how it reacts to the observation. Do this for about ten minutes each day, and be sure to record the results in your Galdor-Book. Observe whether *images* or *sounds* predominate in your mind (or an irregular mixture of both). Some will react with a chaotic demonstration of images, voices, sounds, etc., while others may become very still, and yet others may present a more active, yet constant, sensation.

After these first few days, you will know something of the nature of your unbridled mind, and you can begin to train it to do more difficult tasks set out by your will. You will also have begun to realize the divisibility of the self (the watcher) and thought (in this case that which is being watched). In the second phase of this exercise, begin by *latching onto*, and holding a particular thought and watch it, or listen to it. *Do not try to direct or control it.* Allow it to go its own way. Your task is to concentrate on its every movement or sound. Pursue your train of thought wherever it takes you. Energetically and attentively observe the logical and illogical progressions of our thoughts, and take note how some thoughts and images will respond quite negatively to the attention paid to them by evaporating or freezing, while others thrive on the concentration and seem to be able to go on forever— if *allowed*. Here, your work is not to hold the reins in on the thoughts, but to concentrate on observing where it goes.

Begin this phase by watching thoughts for about three minutes and gradually work your way up to about ten minutes.

3) In this exercise you will take what you have learned and use it in an experiment in controlling your thoughts according to your will. The ultimate goal is to suppress all thought processes, all sounds and images, into a dimensionless and timeless void of consciousness— which is filled with *every* potentiality.

This *stead of timeless stillness* may be reached by subordinating all image to one image, and all sounds to one sound. The image is the bright point, and the sound is that of a runic vowel (usually the "o" or "i" is used). Begin by setting up some object to serve as your bright point— a candle flame, or its reflection in a dish of ink or on an opaque smooth convex surface is excellent. Even more traditional methods are the reflection of the sun or moon in liquid, or on the blade of your sax (Rune-knife), or direct contemplation of the Pole Star. Also, for a fine line rather than a point, the sharp edge of your sax is good. The use of a sharp edge (angle) for making contact with other worlds is well known in Nordic lore. (See J. Simpson *Icelandic Folktales and Legends*, pp. 176-177). Any of these mechanics should, of course, be set up before you begin the exercises, so as not to disturb the flow of the whole. Or you may, if you are able, simply visualize a point of brightness in a black space and concentrate on that. In any event, concentrate on the image of the bright point and mentally hear the continuous vowel sound. All other images are burned away by the point and all sounds are swallowed up by the vowel. Mark well your results in the exercise in the Galdor-Book.

The aim of this work of the stead of stillness is to help the Runer gain some knowledge of the magical place within himself or herself. The results of this will vary from person to person— they can be quite dramatic. If you find the icy stead of stillness and are able to enter into it of any length of time it will be unmistakable. However, future Gild-work may be necessary before this point is fully attained

Another exercise of this type which you might want to take up at this time is the production of a *thought vacuum*. This is actually the twin concept of the stead of stillness (the point). In this work, you are to concentrate on a void-nothingness. To do this, first imagine yourself — your mind — as the limits of all known space, and then empty that space of all sound and image. Now imagine that any sound or word, light or image entering that space is at once burned up, snatched away by the talons of the great eagle— before it even has a chance to manifest itself. This may seem difficult at first, but keep at it and success will follow

You can keep a record of the number of times your concentration is disturbed by using a string of beads (see the section on equipment). As a break in attention occurs, move a bead. After the exercise, you will have a record of the breaks, and one obtained with the least disturbance during the work. This record will also help you assess your day-to-day progress.

For the stead of stillness and the thought-vacuum control exercises you should begin with no more than a minute and eventually work up to five minutes. These may become on-going works which many Runers will wish to return from time to time. As with all concentration-visualization exercises, if you have a day when you just cannot seem to concentrate (and there will be these!) come back the next day and try again for the same length of time (or perhaps a little less) before going on. By the same token, progress may be speedier if you find yourself able to hold your concentration for longer periods, then increase the pace of the time progressions. This is true of anything in the Rune-Gild program.

Rune-Thinking I
(Runic Meditation)

This gives us the tide-clock for the First Door of Midgard. You are, either in your sitting or standing position, to think about the Runes— and dwell on them deeply. In this stage you are free to choose the nature of your meditation. You may concentrate on the name, sound, shape, concepts (one or many), poetic stanza, and any combination of these aspects. The point is to begin to familiarize yourself with the Runes (mysteries) on an inner level. Your mind is given free rein within the broad "limits" of the runic concept to wander and to learn in a direct way. It is only necessary to concentrate on the broad spectrum of the Rune in an intensive way, and to work on vigorously pursuing its meanings and aspects within its own perameters— holding out unrelated distracting thoughts.

Because the meanings of the Runestaves and other aspects basic to Runelore are referred to constantly throughout the Nine Doors, Appendix A has been added to act as a regular reference tool for matters of lore relating to individual Runestaves. This is, however, no substitute for the broader knowledge found in *Runelore* or *Futhark*.

In Rune-Thinking you will follow certain Rune- and time-schedules throughout the 108 days it will take to go through Runes ᚠ/1 - ᚻ/12. The work of each Rune will take nine days. That is, you will spend nine days on *fehu*, nine days on *ūruz*, etc. These exercises will follow the time schedule of 5-6-6-7-8-8-9-10-10 minutes, so that the schedule of any one Rune would look:

day 1 — 5 minutes
day 2 — 6 minutes
day 3 — 6 minutes
day 4 — 7 minutes
day 5 — 8 minutes
day 6 — 8 minutes
day 7 — 9 minutes
day 8 — 10 minutes
day 9 — 10 minutes

This schedule is then to be repeated for each Rune. (The construction of such schedules is perhaps a good habit to get into for various aspects of your training.)

Some type of timer (for example a kitchen timer) is useful to measure the length of the exercises, while the string of beads (see below) is also helpful if you want to begin keeping track of breaks in concentration (when the mind wanders off the path) in an unobtrusive way. This is also a way to help get the mind back on the right road in a gentle, yet firm, way. Each time a break occurs, just move one bead over on the tether, then after the exercise, when it is time to record the day's work, an objective assessment is possible.

This is also a good time to begin learning the relevant stanzas of the various Rune poems (Old English, Old Norwegian, and Old Icelandic). When you are on ᚠ/1 learn the corresponding stanza of each of the Rune poems— you may even make this a part of your meditative work.

The texts of the poems are found in the Third Door. They are also available in their original language on the *Rune-Song* tape, and most importantly are fully edited with glossaries in the volume *The Rune-Poems I* (Rûna-Raven, 2002).

For Runers who, through previous Work, have developed a high level of skill in concentration / visualization the schedule of Rune-Thinking can be accelerated. Advanced students may spend only three days on each Rune (spending ten minutes on each). This would mean the Work of this Door could be reduced to 36 days. Intermediate students could reduce the amount of days spent on each Rune to six (using a schedule of 6-7-8-9-10-10 minutes on each). This would reduce the total number of days for this Door to 72. Such modifications are possible throughout the Nine Doors program— but rigorous self-honesty is needed to create such reschedulings.

There is actually more to the Work than the scheduled Rune-Thinking. Remember that part of the Work is also to absorb and internalize not only the magical content of the Runes but also the basic and essential background lore (information in the suggested readings).

Staða-Work 1

The use of symbolic bodily postures in the practice of magic is well known in many cultures. The most famous of these is the *hatha-yoga* of the Indians. A similar, but simpler, practice was probably also developed by the western Indo-Europeans. Evidence for this in ancient times is rather sparse. What we do have are random clues such as the symbolic (runic?) postures of the figures on the Horns of Gallehus as shown in Figure 1.1:

Figure 1.1: Detail from One of the Two Horns of Gallehus

The fact that the *staða* (posture) of the S-rune involves bending of the knees, and a name of that Rune in Old Icelandic is *knésól* (knee-sun) is significant. As is the modern Icelandic practice of teaching children the alphabet by having them strike postures imitative of the letter shapes.

The practice of runic posture magic — *staðagaldr* — was revived in the early 20th century by the German magicians Friedrich Bernhard Marby and Siegfried Adolf Kummer under the headings of *Runengymnasitk* (runic gymnastics) and *Runenyoga* (runic yoga) respectively. We prefer the more traditional sounding Old Norse term, however. The keys provided by the work of the German masters have, nevertheless, proven to be invaluable aids in the development of the current runic revival— which is not yet finished!

The whole world of the German runic magicians is explored in my book *Rune-Might*.

Our purpose in this first exercise is to begin preparing the body to become a living receiver-transmitter for runic forces, and a proper vessel for the generation and storage of those forces. Here, we will learn to perceive the body as an aspect of a holistic psychophysical (soul-body) complex and to infuse it with consciousness.

First establish a regular rhythm of breath (for example, 5-5-5-5) while maintaining a comfortable and relaxed posture. This should nevertheless be one which demands *attention*. This may be either sitting in a straight-backed chair or sitting in a cross-legged position, or standing erect with your arms at your sides (I-rune *staða*). Eventually you will want to use the standing practice since most *rúnastöður* will work from this posture.

Your task in this exercise is merely to hold the posture in a relaxed, yet poised, attitude, without twitching or jerking— sometimes this is not as easy as it sounds. Also, the Runer should concentrate totally on the posture and the sensations he or she experiences. Practice by moving your attention to various parts of your body in a regular fashion, as well as periodically "perceiving the whole." You should concentrate only on the rhythm of your breath and your posture, but this is not so strictly observed at this stage as in the concentration-visualization exercises above.

Keep a record of your daily progress and any thoughts that might occur during the this work. Begin with about two minutes per day, adding 30 seconds every two days until you have built up to 10 minutes and hold there while refining your abilities.

Rune Tools

The basic tools that you will need for the work of the Nine Doors are for the most part outlined in *Futhark*, pp. 83ff. For actual members of the Rune-Gild, because of the oaths of the Gild, the most important items are the gand (wand) and the sax (knife).

The string of beads mentioned above can be made easily from a leather thong and 24 wooden beads strung upon the thong— but be sure to leave plenty of room (a foot or so) to allow you to move the beads back and forth. This instrument will prove valuable in many kinds of workings.

There are some other items you will need. You will want to get a timer (such as a kitchen timer) to time your exercises without having to "watch the clock." The digital types are especially useful since they are silent. A black cloth about 9″ x 9″, a notebook or blank book to serve as your Galdor-Book, and plenty of candles or an oil lamp for illumination complete the special kinds of tools you will need to get started.

The Other Door of Midgard

On the Gild Concept

In order to preserve and to reflect ancient organizational principles, our society is called a *gild* (we prefer the more archaic English/Norse spelling to the Francisized spelling "guild") and not an *order*. Both concepts share some characteristics, but each has its own unique features as well. The Latin term that corresponds to *gild* is *collegium*, which, of course, gives us the word college. *Order* entered our language through Church Latin and at first referred to ecclesiastical orders, and so forth.

When most people hear the term *gild*, they probably think of *trade* guilds. This is a good start toward understanding the depth of the gild concept. Trade guilds are set up 1) to educate and train persons in certain crafts and skills, and 2) to preserve and to improve this knowledge among members of the gild. This latter point is important. Guild members, once trained, would swear only to teach certain designated persons the skills they had learned, thereby restricting this knowledge to relatively small circle. The practical purpose of this is twofold: 1) to protect the *quality* of the knowledge, and 2) to ensure that the prestige and power of the guild was preserved. In order for the system to work, however, the knowledge must be of an exclusive (virtually secret) type. It is one of the responsibilities of the guild to see to it that such knowledge is held in confidence— otherwise the system becomes a farce.

The method of training in the gild-structure is the most obvious, simple, and human of all types. It is also the only true form of education. A novice or neophyte is chosen based upon factors particular to the nature of the guild, and is initiated as an *apprentice*, whereupon his studies in the craft begin. He is taught by a master, who has also gone through the same training by a *master* before him. After his basic training is complete and he is proven competent in the craft, the apprentice is initiated to the level of *journeyman*. This title is quite descriptive in that the leaner must now leave his master and wander through the land and practice under the guidance of several other masters. At the conclusion of this period, after the journeyman has refined his skills, he presents evidence of this skill in tangible form— the so-called master-piece. This is really a *piece* of work which gives evidence of his *mastery* in the craft. This piece of work is judged by a group of masters, and if it is found worthy, he is recognized and initiated as a master of the guild. It then becomes his right and obligation to teach other apprentices and journeymen the skills of the craft.

This pattern is clear in all guild-based institutions. Not only did manufacture of goods come under this system, but also all training in intellectual or other skills. Warriors were taught their ways and magicians their craft according to the same system. The transmission of intellectual skills in this method came to be known as a *university* (or *college*) system.

Before applying these principles to the Rune-Gild, the deepest level of meaning for the term *gild* must be explored. Although the general system itself is virtually universal, the Germanic term ultimately refers to a specific type of institution. The Common Germanic **geldjōn* originally meant a payment, that is, "something *given*," and hence it is attached to an institution established for the *giving of gifts* (sacrifices) to the gods. The first gilds were then associations formed for the performance of cultic rites— which could sometimes be quite complex. The *giving* involved in the gild belongs to an ecology of power in which brothers and sisters in the gild "yield" (a word cognate to gild) offerings to the institution, which are in turn yielded to the god of the gild in a collective manner, and from this yielding the body of the gild receives the blessings of the god.

The original trade or craft guilds probably developed from these god-gilds in that certain skills which came under the domain of a god or goddess would be taught within the gild of that god or goddess. The religious nature of these institutions in pagan times were then carried over into Christian times as well. Guilds took on patron saints and had special guild feasts for them (in place of the ancient divine blessings) and there ever developed purely religious guilds dedicated to certain saints. The basic structure of their rites and practices, and a good deal of their ideology, remained pre-Christian, however. It is in this context that the guild of Free-Masons (stone masons, brick-layers, etc.) developed in the direction they did.

Every guild works in some *substance* or another— the cobbler works in leather to fashion shoes, the tailor in cloth to make clothes. In the Rune-Gild the complex essence in which we work in the Self, the ultimate product of our work is the Erulian. It is important to the maintenance of the quality of individual "products," and of the collective whole, that the methods of the gild and its rituals — such as they are known to any one Gilder — be kept secret from outsiders. Diffusion of these forms would only lead to the dissipation of their power. However, it is our advantage that the true secrets are contained in the essence *behind* the forms— the forms themselves are pathways or tools toward the realization of the essence. Therefore, should our secrets ever be disseminated by an untrue Gilder — and after the betrayer(s) had been weeded out by the magical act of will — the Rune-Masters of the Gild would merely alter the forms thereby invalidating the previous ones and preserving the access to the true essence for true Gilders only. Those in possession of the old forms would just be led into confusion by their ill gotten gains.

The purpose of our Gild is the shaping of selves guided by the Hidden God, Wōden. The shape of each of these selves is unique, as is the way in which Wōden speaks to each of these selves. The Gild and its Rune-Masters can give lore and road-maps, and provide a social framework for the initiation of individuals, and maintain standards in all realms— but it and we can not *do* the work for any individual (nor can we *initiate* an individual in a manner similar to "plugging them in" to our stream). The Wōden within, the essence of the Self, initiates— the Gild recognizes these facts.

To sum up, a gild is a man-made institution for the initiation of individuals into a given system of knowledge and reality. This institution is charged with the responsibility of maintaining a link with the god of that gild and preserving among men and women the quality of the essence of the god and of the craft that is taught within the gild.

Soul-Lore
(Traditional Psychology of the Gild)

The "substance" in which the Runer works is the **soul** or psyche. The soul has become less and less well known in our culture as Christianity (with its primitive and unsophisticated and confused psychology) slowly destroyed our knowledge of our souls and thus of ourselves.

Much of this material is covered in *Runelore* (pp. 167-173) and in *A Book of Troth*. The ambitious reader is also referred to my article "Toward an Archaic Germanic Psychology."

But the ancient psychology of the Germanic peoples is something which, with a good deal of work, can be recovered. This is because ancient Germanic literature is full of references to ideas concerning the soul and how it works in people's live and how it motivates them to action and because we still carry the seeds of this psychology in our very beings today. No amount of negative programming can completely destroy it. It awaits only the right kind of attention to bloom forth again. Such a recovery is necessary for your ultimate progress in the Doors. The various parts of the body-soul complex must be known and understood in order that you can work with them, and we can talk about them in specific ways later.

The ancient Germanic psychology speaks of not a single soul, but a number of them— all making a complex system which all together makes up the whole person. The Old Norse terminology of the soul is the most complete and sophisticated we have in any Germanic language. Therefore, the modernized terms are also given in Old Norse in the descriptions below. A symbolic representation of the whole image is presented in Figure 2.1.

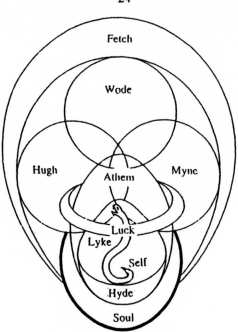

Figure 2.1: The Traditional Body-Soul Complex

The lyke (ON *lík*) is the physical body itself. It is given its shape by the subtle force of the hyde (ON *hamr*). The hyde is the plastic "image-stuff" that gives shape to objects (including the human body) and also that material which can be formed and mutated by the human will. What happens to or in the hyde will be reflected in the lyke.

The athem (ON *önd*) is the "breath of life" the animating principle and the medium for the entry of certain kinds of transpersonal powers into the human psychosomatic (soul-body) complex.

The hugh (ON *hugr*) and myne (ON *minni*) must be treated together. These are the internal reflections or representatives of Wōden's two ravens Huginn and Muninn— "Mind" and "Memory." But that might lead to oversimplification. The hugh, or hidge, is the cognitive faculty— that part of the mind that can analyze and compute data, linguistic or mathematical. Some would equate it with the left hemi-sphere of the brain. The myne is the reflective faculty— that part of the mind that uses images, shapes and dimensions to store and work with the mind's own contents. Certain contents of the myne are **innate** and transpersonal. This is the store-house of the archetypes of the collective unconscious, if you will. Some would equate this part of the mind with the right hemisphere of the brain.

Interlocking with the athem, hugh and myne is the wode (ON *óðr*) or principle of inspiration or enthusiasm. This can have various characters depending on the person. It can express itself in a furious rage or a quiet uplifting of the whole being to a sublime state of poetic and intellectual inspiration. This is the magical faculty by which the contents and activities of the hugh and myne are synthesized.

The hugh, myne and wode touch— but do not fully intersect the fetch (ON *fylgja*) which may be thought to be actually somewhat *independent* of the individual. Some individuals may not even have a fetch, or it may be poorly developed, or very young. Work presented in the latter Doors will show you how to begin to work directly with the fetch. The fetch itself is in some a complex entity— with as many as three aspects: an animal-fetch (there may be more than one of these), a contra-sexual fetch (gender opposite that of the lyke to which it is attached), and an abstract geometrical shape (often a crescent). This is the faculty through which transpersonal powers, gifts, and responsibilities are transmitted, and the faculty in which the person's actions are stored and from which these actions are reflected back in the individual's life.

Sometimes closely related to the fetch in the way it works in an individual's life is the faculty of "luck" (ON *hamingja*). This is a protective essence or substance which is the *power* to cause changes in the hyde-substance in the world. It is the faculty used in true shape-shifting, a craft that has been lost with the perfect knowledge of the soul.

The soul itself is technically the shade of a person after he or she dies. It is the soul concept that becomes the postmortem body— which awaits rebirth from one of the abodes of the dead.

Finally the self is (potentially) the faculty for the synthesis and understanding of all the other faculties and essences. Some may only know little of this whole complex— and thus have a limited self. The *ego*, or simply and rightly put, the I-consciousness, is usually located at the apex of the lyke/self— with some access to the athem, hugh and myne. The inspired or magically developed self, which has been developed through Rune-Work rises to the intersection of the wode, hugh, myne and athem. This is the wode-self, which is a higher form of yourself, a higher ego-consciousness.

— Opening —

As you embark through the Other Door of Midgard you should stay with your general daily plan of Rune-Work. Make only those changes that are necessary to your regularizing of the work. It is important that you be efficient with your time so that the work does not begin to take up more space in the day than you are willing and able to give to it. Do not give yourself any excuse to work less than you should. Many will feel that regular work of the kind outlined in the Doors of Midgard is drudgery. It can be if it is not constantly being *put to use*. The Gild-

Work is the skeleton of an initiatory runic system, but all Runers have the obligation to flesh out those bones with their own magical workings. Our tradition is a rich one — as all of you know — but there is also a deep tradition of innovation and adaptation in Germanic Runelore. As you learn more of the *essence* of the Runes you will be able to innovate in an authentic manner. The urge to invent or adapt from other traditions should be held in check in the early stages— until the true essence is grasped. At this juncture, many will want to begin fleshing out their work with magical experiments of various kinds. The book *Futhark* gives a fair variety of these. You may also wish to begin working with staves for oracular or divinatory purposes. *Runecaster's Handbook* gives ample indications of how you could go about this. All of these topics will be covered in greater detail in the course of the Nine Doors. Divination is taken up on a theoretical basis in this Door, and in the next Door we will start with practical work. In any case, it is our rede to you that you should, if you have not already, begin supplementing your regular Rune-Gild work with various kinds of experiments (ritual or otherwise) that are designed for your own *personal* aims. This will keep motivation at a higher level.

This Door, as with the First, should take about 108 days to complete.

Reading

Suggested reading for the Other Door:
The Psychology of Man's Possible Evolution, P. D. Ouspensky
"Toward an Archaic Germanic Psychology," Stephen E. Flowers
The Master Game, Robert S. De Ropp
Occult Exercises and Practices, Gareth Knight
The Poetic Edda, Lee M. Hollander (tr.)
The Prose Edda, Snorri Sturluson
Gods of the Ancient Northmen, Georges Dumézil
The New Comparative Mythology, C. Scott Littleton
The Road to Hel, H.R. Ellis (Davidson)
Myth and Religion of the North, E.O.G. Turville-Petre
"A Semiotic Theory of Rune-Magic" in *Studia Germanica I*, Stephen E. Flowers
The Saga of the Volsungs, Jesse Byock (tr.)
"Is Sigurðr Sigmundr *aptrborinn*?" in *Studia Germanica I*, Stephen E. Flowers
The Psychology of C.G. Jung, Jolande Jacobi
The Archetypes and the Collective Unconscious, C.G. Jung
"Some Socio-Cultic Aspects of the Runes during the Migration Age" in *Studia Germanica I*, Stephen E. Flowers

WORKINGS

Continue with the Daily Workings of opening and closing your formal work with these formulas.

To the Daily Rite of Dedication, or opening formula, you are now to add one of the following forms of the runic hammer-signing.

I: The All-Gods Form of Hammer-Signing

Stand erect, facing north; settle breathing to a steady rhythm and visualize at arm's length above your head a swirling, glowing mass of golden-white energy— in the midst of which if the "trifos" or triskelion . With your open right hand reach aloft and grasp the center of the mass — making a fist in the middle of it — and bring it down to a point just in front of your forehead. As you do this, you will draw down a column of energy through the center of your being. Stop there and say:

Týr / Tiw or Tiwaz

touching the point between your eyes with the fist knuckle of your thumb— a fifth of the energy enters your head and fills your skull with brilliant powers. Now bring your fist down to a point just in front of the top of your sternum. Stop there and say:

Óðinn / Wōden or Wōðanaz

touching the top of the sternum — a fifth of the power flows into your chest and throat and fills your upper body with shining force. Now continue downward and draw the column of light to the solar plexus. Touch that point at the bottom of the sternum and say:

Þórr / Þunor or Þunaraz

From this blazing center the force moves to the core of your being. Move your fist to your left shoulder, touch it saying the name:

Freyja / Frēo or Fraujōn

and pull a line of shining energy across your heart to your right shoulder. Touch it with the name:

Freyr / Frēa or Fraujaz

Drop your arm to your side and concentrate on the hammer-pattern of force you have called into being in your body as seen in Figure 2.2.

Note: The names given above are the Old Norse, Old English and Proto-Germanic forms of the divine names.

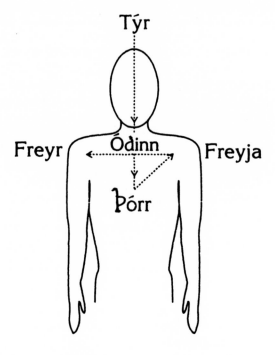

Figure 2.2: The All-Gods Form of the Hammer-Signing

The theological pattern is, of course, the most ancient trifunctional pantheon made clear in the work of Georges Dumézil.

II: The Odian Form of the Hammer-Signing
Follow the same general pattern as above with the names as follows:

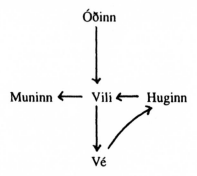

Figure 2.3: Tracing of the Hammer-Sign

This is an especially potent formula for the calling up of the Wōdenic stream within the self— for it causes us to identify clearly with the godly image of our Gild Drighten.

The overall functions of the hammer-working are, 1) to balance the energy levels in the body in preparation for work, and 2) to call upon the archetypal and ancestral forces to fill our beings for this work. The first form of the rite may also be employed to bless other objects or persons, however, the second form may only be used subjectively. I think all will understand why.

The Hammer-Working

To project the Hammer of Þórr into the objective universe around you to act as a way of "protecting" your field of working from distracting intrusions, you can perform the Hammer-Working.

1. Face North.

2. Starting with *fehu* in the North, trace the shapes of the Runestaves in a ring around you at the level of your solar plexus. The ring should be about three to four feet away from you in the air. When you are finished you will end with the sign of *ōþala* also in the north right next to the sign of *fehu*, and the Runes will form a complete band around you.

3. Stand in the cross-position (with your arms straight out from your sides) and visualize an equilateral cross lying horizontally in the plane of the Rune ring and your solar plexus— which will be the very center of that cross. The arms of the cross will end at the points where they touch the Rune band. Imagine a surrounding sphere of shimmering blue light with the red Rune-band as its equator. Then visualize the vertical axis coming through your length from infinite space above and from the infinite space below you.

4. Feel the force flowing into your center from all six directions as it builds a sphere of glowing red might. The color may be altered depending on the ritual intention.

5. The Runer should touch the hinder part of the gand to the breast at the center of power and thrust it forward, projecting the force from that center to a point on the inside face of the outer sphere. Then the Runer should sign the hammer ⊥ from the mass of magical might gathered and visualized at that point. The sign should be traced as shown in Figure 2.3. During this process intone:

Hamarr í Norðri helga vé þetta ok hald vörð!

(Hammer in the North hallow and hold this holy stead!)

Then turning 90 degrees to the right trace again the hammer sign in the east, saying:

Hamarr í Austri helga vé þetta ok hald vörð!

(Hammer in the East hallow and hold this holy stead!)

Then turning 90 degrees to the right again trace the hammer sign in the south and say:

Hamarr í Suðri helga vé þetta ok hald vörð!

(Hammer in the South hallow and hold this holy stead!)

And turning to the West, say:

Hamarr í Vestri helga vé þetta ok hald vörð!

(Hammer in the West hallow and hold this holy stead!)

Returning to the north, direct your attention upward and there directly overhead, at the apex of the sphere, trace the sign of the hammer, saying:

Hamarr yfir mér helga vé þetta ok hald vörð!

(Hammer above me hallow and hold this holy stead!)

And then project the hammer sign below to the nadir of the sphere and say:

Hamarr undir mér helga vé þetta ok hald vörð!

(Hammer under me hallow and hold this holy stead!)

6. Now assume the cross position again and say:

Hamarr helga vé þetta ok hald vörð!

(Hammer hallow and hold this holy stead!)

Turning in the center of the ring repeat this for each of the other four directions and once for the vertical axis. The visual effect should be one of axes connecting all six shining red hammers to your personal center, all engulfed by a field of sparkling deep blue light and surrounded by the band of bright red Runes.

7. Center all the forces in the ring by folding your arms from the cross position toward your center, with your fingertips touching your solar plexus, saying:

Um mik ok í mér Ásgarðr ok Miðgarðr!

(Around me and in me Asgard and Midgard!)

This ritual may be used at any time to balance and protect you and to hallow any place by the power of Thunar's Hammer.

It should be noted that if you have a stead of working which is *permanently hallowed*— a holy-stead reserved for holy work, such as your own grove, hof or hall, then workings such as the Hammer-Working are *not necessary*. They *can* become redundant and even counter-productive.

Tracing of the Hammer-Sign

Two general workings that have proven effective may also be instituted at this time. They are the "washing stave" and the "meal stave."

The Washing Stave: (Fill the sink or a large bowl with cold water, and wash your face, neck, and chest with this water, repeating this stave, or a similar formula.):

I wash myself in thy might and in thy blood and in thy seed o great Gaut!1) I wash away all ill-will that dwelled within me and without me — away it runs as ice struck by the great golden sow2) — away ill-will, out with evil and ill-health — I bear the helm of awe3) on my brow between my eyes and with its might all evil is stemmed and stopped— as its power streams through my body!

The Meal Stave: Before eating or drinking you may bless the food or drink by holding both hands over them, making the *höndstaða* of the Ing-rune (:◊:) with the finger tips and thumbs and say:

(Eating)
Food of life filled with the might and main of Yngvi-Freyr— give me the energy this day that I may work my will — Weal-Will-Wealth fills every fiber of my being.
(Drinking)
Drink of power, loaded with the force of life— flow into me and fill my being with energy without bound!

Personal Analysis Diary II
(Life-Work)

Now that you have established your exhaustive list of bright and murky — you will want to begin to manipulate these characteristics according to your will. This will be an ongoing process. After all, the learning of what one's true will actually is may be another task altogether. But at this point, you may begin to assign your various characteristics to Runestaves. For this the runic correspondences and interpretations given in *Futhark* will be of great help.

Let us say you have "laziness" on your murky list. This is a form of psychic entropy, and so is to be ascribed to the *isa*-rune as a constriction of energy. On the other hand, you may have "powers of concentration" on your bright list— this would also be ascribed to the

---

1)Wōden, 2)Sunna (the sun), 3)At this point draw the helm of awe (*ægishjálmr*) between your eyes: ⌁

isa-rune. The difference lies, of course, in the question of will and in the matter of the *focal point* of that "concentration" of energy— inactivity or an object of work/contemplation. Go through your list of characteristics and ascribe a stave or *staves* (certain complex traits may require the construction of specific bind-runes) to them. Do this with care and deliberation. This activity itself constitutes an act of meditative work in which much of the essence of your inner self will be revealed to you.

After you have completed this, turn your attention to the investigation of your true will. This is not a task for which any single method is possible. It is a work that may be done quickly for some, but for others there may be a great struggle and quest. Do not necessarily expect or desire quick results— here as everywhere only truth is important. You should make this an ongoing project until you are satisfied with the results. Methods you will use in this investigation would include meditation and divination. Turn inward to yourself for guidance, turn toward your fetch and to your gods and goddesses for holy rede. Learn your destiny and fulfill it— this is a great rede and high. Further guidance is available on an individual basis to Rune-Gilders who may have need of it— but outside advice should only be used in carefully chosen circumstances. The best council always comes from within your own being, and outside council should only be used to corroborate findings or help make refinements or decisions among pre-determined possibilities.

Vocalic Breathing II
In the second stage of vocalic breathing we will deepen the level of practice of what we have begun, expand on the work, and meld it into the practice of the Yew-Working (see below).

1) Continue the repeated practice of individual vocalic sounds. Work on a single vowel per day. Day 1: A, day 2: U, etc. Each session of vocalic breathing should last from between 5 and 10 minutes. Go through all five vowels five times (= a total of 25 days).

2) Now, go back to the cyclical multi-vocalic system in the variant sequences A.U.E.I.O. and U.A.I.E.O. This is also known as the "wave pattern"— the feelings evoked by this practice should tell you why. Do this for an additional 25 days.

3) Next comes a new dimension. Now, *add* consonants to the vowels. There are 18 consonants in the runic system:
f.þ.r.k.g.w.h.n.j.p.z.s.t.b.m.l.ng.d.
You should attach the five main vowel sounds to each of the consonants in turn, for example:
fa fu fe fi fo
af uf ef if of

Experiment with the repeated individual articulation of vowel-consonant combinations and with the "wave method." Spend two days on each combination except F and D which should get three days each (= 38 days). Remain totally concentrated on *technique* at this point. Of course, all of these sounds have runic correspondences— and we will get to their further practical application and significance soon enough.

Preliminaries to the Yew-Working

For the last 20 days of the Other Door, you will conduct exercises in preparation for the Yew-Working. This is one of the most profound of the Gild's works. In these 20 days, the work of vocalic breathing and the *staða* work (see below) are brought together— where they ultimately belong. We will, however, continue to cultivate the art of galdor independent of the standings (*stöður*) This corresponds to the *Staða*-Work II B and C below.

Staða-Work II

(A)

Now, if you have not already, you will move from a sitting or lying posture to a standing one for your exercises. Stand erect, with arms relaxed at your sides, and your feet at a 90-degree angle:

90 Degrees

Hold this position without twitching or jerking for 10 minutes, with deep concentration on the rhythm of your breath. Do this daily for 68 days. Think of the essence of "ice."

(B)

At the end of the 68 days in the silent I-rune standing— begin to practice the true EI-rune standing. Stand on your right foot, with your left calf bent up at a 45-degree angle (facing north):

Practice this standing for 20 days. You will have to concentrate on holding your balance. But skills gained in the 68 days of *isa* will have steeled you well. Do the standing progressively from 3 to 10 minutes daily.

(C)

Now go back to the more relaxed I-rune standing for the inclusion of the EI-galdor. This vowel sound is somewhat akin to the "a" in English "ash." Feel a state of relaxation throughout your whole physical being during these 20 five to ten minute sessions. Concentrate on the shape of the EI-rune running through your body from the bottom of your feet to the top of your head. It is shining, but colorless.

The next Door will contain a deep level extension of this practice that will provide the hidden key to how *rúnastöður* can be made to work in a much more conscious fashion. This will also provide a key to the psychophysical mysteries of Germanic tree-symbolism.

Concentration-Visualization II

1) Here, you will wish to shape a set of runic "meditational cards," that is images of the Runestaves upon which to concentrate. These can be of virtually any size (5″x3″ would be about the minimum), but the Runes should be painted in *red*. The background may be white, blue or green. The card should be displayed at eye level and about as far away as five times the height. For example, if your stave is 6″ high, it should be about 30″ away.

Begin with the Rune that you find most appealing visually. Concentrate on its *form* as it stands before you. Spend five minutes in this, then close your eyes and see it in your mind's eye. Concentrate on all its angles and segments— hold its image in your *hugauga* (your mind's eye) for up to 10 minutes. You will incrementally be able to decrease the amount of time you spend concentrating on the form with the physical eye so that the whole operation should take no more than 10 minutes. Hold to a schedule, but keep it flexible. The idea is to be able to hold the simple, static, Runestave in the mind's eye for 10 minutes. You may change Runes, or do a different one every day if variety helps your concentration.

Do this simple form of runic concentration-visualization for 54 days.

2) In the next 54 days, add two other (any two other) Runes to the session. Display the three cards before yourself and repeat the general procedure as with one single Rune. The Runes you choose should be harmoniously related in essence and/or shape. Some examples might be:

  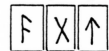

You may work with one triad, or experiment with several as you feel appropriate. During each session concentrate on each in turn individually, and in various orders. *See* the interrelationships between and among the Runestaves. You may wish to start over with a schedule of 5 minutes, working up to an intensive 10 minutes.

Rune-Thinking II
(Runic Meditation)

This is a continuation from the first half of the fuþark. Follow the same general plan outlined in Rune-Thinking I in the First Door. The only alteration you might wish to make is a speeding up or the lengthening of each Rune-session. You may find that now it is quite easy for you to spend close to 10 minutes in runic meditation from day one of each Rune. In any event, you should stick to the schedule of spending an even number of days on each Rune so that 108 days will be spend on Runes ↑/13-↗/24.

Certainly by now you should be quite familiar with the contents of all the Rune poems. In the next Door we will begin to "internalize" them.

The Theory of Rune-Galdor

At this point, you may or may not feel that it is necessary to have a "theory" about what Rune galdor is and how it works. Although it is not absolutely necessary at this point in your development, the high Rede would be somewhat disappointed if you were not in some way *seeking* an explanation of the mystery of galdor. It should be in the very essence of the Odian to seek the *hidden principles* of everything. This particular topic is a vast one— and it may take some years of work to come to a comprehensive understanding of it. But you do not need to understand all of the details of the construction of the internal combustion engine to drive a car... In any event, in the next few pages we will outline a theory of magical principles which is in general agreement with many of the most advanced and current anthropological theories of magic and at the same time one that is significantly advanced over most "superstitious" type theories of magic found in many occult schools and "religions" today. The reader is especially referred to my article "A Semiotic Theory of Rune Magic" found in the volume *Studia Germanica I*.

The Runes

For a general discussion of the nature of the Runes and the word "Rune," the reader is referred to both *Futhark* and *Runelore*. Here, I want to delve well beyond the primary esoteric meaning "secret," or "mystery" and come to a deeper understanding of that essence.

The principal question stands: Is a "Rune" an essence existing in the objective universe, or is it an artificial construct of the psyche (that is, of the subjective universe)? By the *objective* universe we mean the natural/organic/mechanical world outside the sphere of human consciousness— that is, all that is not in possession of the gifts of Wōðanaz-Wiljōn-Wīhaz. By the *subjective* universe we mean all that is in possession of these gifts— that is, human consciousness— and most particularly that "spark" of the gift of Wōðanaz which *you* possess. (Remember *you* have the gifts, the gifts do not have you! The objective universe is the environment external to all that you are conscious of as being "you," the subjective universe is all that is internal to that same model. There is also the concept of the world, or the whole universe, which is the entirety of existence both the subjective and objective, known and unknown.

Now, it is generally held that the Runes are "cosmic mysteries"— and thus it would seem that they have existence in the objective universe— which indeed they do. However, they are more particularly the principles of consciousness— the framework or structure of consciousness, if you will. And here is the key concept: Since the Runes are an objective structure of *consciousness* it is precisely in that realm (of consciousness) that the Runes are most accessible to us. Wōden gave us the Runes in latent forms— but we must emulate his primal act of Rune-winning to make them real *for ourselves*. Therefore, the Runes are subjective patterns that are reflections of objective principles or forms which must be *made real* by the will or consciousness of the Runer. The reality of the Runes is to be found in the essence of the gifts of Wōden (of which the Runes are a road-map). Their reality is demonstrated by the very *ability* of the Runer to be the artificer of his own reality— which is part of the essence of "magic."

From this it can be seen why these patterns were designated as "mysteries" (Runes). Because they are the very core of consciousness it is virtually impossible for the self to objectify them completely. This will become clearer as more subjective magical work is undertaken. This is why, for us, it is so important to remain true to the ancient *traditional forms* of the Runes. These forms are firm anchors in the objective universe upon which we can confidently build. Other pseudo-runic systems are the pure constructs of the subjective universes of their creators. As such, they only have the reality which you are willing to grant them.

The division of reality into a "subjective" and "objective" sphere is a model of understanding which does not necessarily correspond to anything with absolute validity. it is rather a working model or poetic paradigm with which the creative mind of the practitioner of galdor works.

Fig. 2.4: The Runes of the Subjective and Objective Universes

Galdor

After we can clearly see the objective universe and the subjective universe we will be able to undertake true galdor. One of the main reasons for this ability is that once you become aware of the objective universe and its mechanical/organic (natural) characteristics and of the subjective universe (as the many halled structure of your psychophysical complex)— you at once awaken to the fact that the "one" which *is aware* of these things is something distinct and separate from either. This is the Self— the self-aware consciousness. Once this realization is reached *galdor* (that is, the engineering of the objective and subjective universes in accordance with the *will* of that self) is possible. "Magic" is then the causing of changes to occur in the subjective or objective universes in accordance with the will of the self.

Of course, this "will" and this "self," if it has evolved to a point approaching the *ginnregin*, or the advising gods, will not be found to be something wildly at odds with the traditional values and sensibilities of what is considered a "right" or "fitting" action or state of being. This is why the most ancient of examples of rune-magic (the older runic inscriptions) never have the typical contents of magical formulas in more decadent societies.

In any event, how is this performed by means of the Runes? In an essential way, *all* galdor is effected through Runes in the sense that they are (in our tradition) the structures of consciousness— and consciousness is the realm in which galdor is effected. However, more specifically, galdor may be viewed as a *system of communication* between the subjective and objective universes. And quite "simply" the Runes are the means of this "inter-reality communication."

In a Rune-working the subjective Rune-realms are craftily engineered (through a myriad of techniques) in accordance with the willed objectives of the Runer. In these subjective Rune-realms a link, a galdor-ring, is forged with the corresponding patterns in the objective Rune-realms; and thus, if the impression is strong enough, the corresponding patterns will emerge in the objective universe. Thus the change is wrought. This process can also, of course, be used to change one or another part of the subjective universe to accord with the will of the self. This is the essence of self-transformation— the work central to the Gild.

Put perhaps in over-simplistic terms, galdor is a system of communication whereby the subjective consciousness of the Runer is able to "converse with" the objective and/or various parts of his or her own subjective universe.

Just by way of simple example, let us say that you wish to attract some deal of money to yourself. The first step would consist of loading the appropriate Rune ($\mathnormal{F}$) with the value of "wealth." This is not fully intrinsic to the stave shape/name, etc.— it is your *work* to make the stave which is traditionally predisposed in this direction *alive* with the corresponding power. This whole process is much of the essence of the Gild-work you are now doing. Now, the Rune is ready to be used by you. By any one or combination of a number of techniques (see *Futhark*) the Runer can impress the Runes onto the subjective universe. During the working, the Runestave is linked with its corresponding objective counterpart (by means of the magical link phenomenon)— and released to do its work in the objective universe. By this method the subjective, and thus the objective universe, is programmed with *fehu*— and this force (Rune), as you have encoded it, is then impressed into the objective universe.

By this technique the objective universe is "brought into tune" with your subjective program. The point of galdor is to bring the objective world (and peripheral areas of the subjective world) into accord with your*self*-determined, willed, conscious plans. This is distinguished from "religion" (as commonly understood) by the fact that most religions have a pre-set plan for the adherent to follow. Deviation from the plan is called "sin," and the follower is considered virtuous insofar as he or she fulfills "god's will" that is, that of the mechanical, monolithic cosmos. This is not the path of the Odian. The essence of our path is the discovery of self and the transformation of self in accordance with will.

But why *Runes* and not Chinese characters or Egyptian hieroglyphics? Most Gilders know the answer here. Because we are *of* Wōden (descended from him as our ancestral sovereign god-head) it is through his gifts — in their *original* forms — that we will most easily gain access to the hidden magical realms of ourselves and of the objective universe. The Runer is a wolf of the spirit — he will never take difficult prey when easy prey is lying before him. The Runes are already encoded in us— more than find them we must *awaken* what we already possess.

Although the Runes lie — more or less dormant in the beginning — within a number of men and women who have been touched by the gifts of Wōden, it is up to each individual to make the Runes real for himself. This is an integral part of the true process. The "Runes" will not come swooping out of the sky and take over your being— they would thereby loose their validity as patterns of *self*-aware consciousness. No, the runic realms within the self must not *do the work*. This is the process that the Nine Doors is all about. The Runes must be internalized— made your own by a process of conscious will. The forms exist within you— but *you* must make them live. The Runestaves have been cut— but you must now stain them with thine own blood.

All of what has been written here has been learned in light of the Words of the High One:

> I know that I hung   on the windy tree
>   all of nights nine,
> wounded by gar,   given to Óðinn,
>   myself to myself,
> upon that tree   of which none can tell
>   from what roots it rises.

It is this process of "giving self to self" that true Rune-galdor is all about.

The Third Door of Midgard
— Opening —

You are now passing through the Third Door of Midgard. In all this Door should take 240 days to complete. This is a time of consolidating skills and developing new techniques. You should continue to be regular in your work. However, at this juncture a word of wisdom must be spoken. Surely not all Runers can keep to this rigid schedule— and indeed there will be those times when you can not undertake any work at all. Also, there will be those times when in one hour of work — or even in a single intense minute — you will accomplish a week's or a year's worth of growth. The point is that you *grow*— the High Rede will *know* that you have grown through the communications you send to us. Remember your Gild-Work is manifold— it is intellectual, it is numinous, it is emotional, it is physical. All must grow evenly— or as evenly as your self will allow.

Reading

Suggested reading of the Third Door:

The Galdrabók, Stephen E. Flowers (ed.)
*Northern Magic, Edred
*Runecaster's Handbook, Edred
*Rúnarmál I, Stephen E. Flowers
*Green Rûna, Edred
*The Rune-Poems I, Stephen E. Flowers
Icelandic Folktales and Legends, Jacqueline Simpson
Legends of Icelandic Magicians, Jacqueline Simpson
The Penguin Book of Scandinavian Folktales, Jacqueline Simpson
Skaldic Number-Lore, Robert Zoller
Towards a Germanic Esoteric Astronomy, Robert Zoller

The Lore of the Yggdrasill
(Principles of Runic Cosmology)

Runic cosmology is covered in some detail in *Runelore* (chapter 10) which you should have already studied. Now is the time to review this lore and to begin to weave it together with the lore of the soul. Our purpose here is to learn as much about how the world and the soul are seen to work together in like ways in the Germanic philosophy.

The basic structure of Yggdrasill is shown in Figure 3.1. We see that there is a vertical axis of being containing five levels bisected by a plane of four fields of force or energy. These make up the nine worlds of Yggdrasill. This whole model is envisioned as being *dynamic*. The four fields of force orbit the central axis, and there are vertical flows of substance up and down the central column— from the "roots" to the "branches" and back again. It can be seen how the Yggdrasill model is the true image of the workings of a tree of cosmic proportions.

Each of the nine worlds has a separate identity, each has its own function and reality. But all work together to form the universe as we know it. Throughout the rest of the Nine Doors curriculum you will be exploring these worlds on different levels and from different angles. Right now what is important is that you gain some definite ideas about what each of these worlds means.

The five worlds of the vertical axis are Ásgarðr, Ljóssálfheimr, Miðgarðr, Svartálfheimr, and Hel (or Helheim)

Ásgarðr
(Enclosure of the Æsir)

This is the realm of consciousness— it is a manifold world made up of many halls and houses. Focus on this realm is the highest form of consciousness, which is really a divine state of being. The central hall is Valhöll (or Walhalla) ruled over by the All-Father, Wōden. This is the realm of the synthesis of the spirit— the abode of the fetch and of the wode-self, or "magical persona." Here is the level of the synthesis of the memory of divine existence (myne) and the faculty of the intellect (hugh).

Ljóssálfheimr
(Light-Elf World)

This is the wide expanse of white light also containing manifold levels or sub-strata called halls or abodes. This is the realm form which the brightness of the human intellect (hugh) derives.

Miðgarðr
(The Middle Enclosure)

This is the *central* reality of humanity. The realm where the soul and the body are in a symbiotic state. In objective terms this is the realm of material manifestation— the Earth. This does not represent a geocentric cosmology, but rather one that puts the *here and now* at the center of our attention— and at the center of the god's attention.

Svartálfheimr
(Black-Elf World)

The "black-elves" are really the dwarves— the formative aspects of being. This is the realm of *formation*, of the shape (or hyde) in humanity. All the things in Midgard have their original shape or form in Svartálfheimr.

Hel
(The Realm of the Dead)

This is the abode of the dead— from which the souls undergo rebirth. The dead are ever present and actually nourish the living with their existence. It is the abode of stillness, silence, and inertia. Once it is entered, it is very difficult to leave without great power— usually provided from outside Hel. This is the realm of the goddess Hel, daughter of Loki. Hel is not a place of punishment. It is more like a place of rest or stasis — indeed a state much abhorred by the Germanic mind. From this state it awaits reawakening. The realm of Niflhel which is the "lowest" level of Hel is a place totally lacking in *being*.

The four worlds of the outer force fields are Niflheimr, Muspellsheimr, Vanaheimr, and Jötunheimr.

Niflheimr
(World of Mist)
North

This is the realm of the origin of all waters— waters that become ice. It is the field of magnetism and contraction. Niflheimr is a zone of anti-matter and a realm in which existence as we can envision it is virtually impossible. It is a zone of *negative existence*. This cosmic Niflheimr is not to be confused with Nifl*hel* which is a further "lower" subdivision of Hel itself.

Muspellsheimr
(World of Fire)
South

This is the realm of the fiery sparks and the place of the origin of all forms of positive energy— expansive and electric. This is the outward expanding energy which is drawn to the antimatter of Niflheimr, giving the conditions that make Midgard possible between them. However, existence as we know it is also quite impossible in Muspellsheimr. The beings ascribed to both Niflheimr and Muspellsheimr can only exist on the edges of these worlds— in their cores are intense realms of totally dis-integrative forces— thurses of fire and ice.

Vanaheimr
(Wane-Home)
West

The Wanes (ON Vanir) are the gods and goddesses of productiveness and organic growth. In this realm is the organic patterning of organic existence. This is a world of eternal balance of cyclical nature— there is constant growth here but nothing can be seen to change or really happen here. There is eternal well-being, peace, pleasure and comfort. This is the realm of organic and cosmic as well as personal cycles.

Jötunheimr
(Etin-World)
East

This is the realm of the "giants" (etins). In counter-balance to Vanaheimr, Jötunheimr is a place of constant change. It seeks and its inhabitants seek to oppose and change anything they come up against. But the realm itself can not really undergo its own metamorphosis. It is a catalyst for change and evolution, but can not itself change or evolve. Jötunheimr is a place of dissolution— and possibly deception for those who are unprepared for its "tricks." Jötunheimr is the reactive power of de-struction necessary to evolutionary change.

In course of the coming Doors you will gain more and more access to the mysteries of these worlds in more direct ways. These hints, however, can continue to spark your sense of what these realms represent in the world and within your own self. There is a deep underlying coherence to this system that is directly perceptible in the Yew-Work.

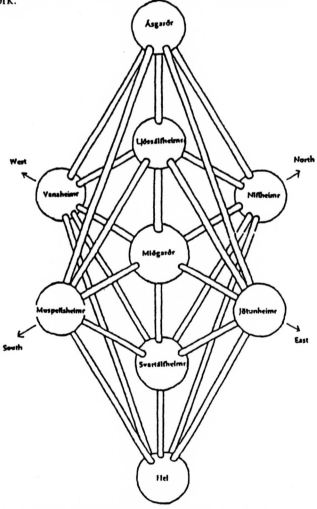

Figure 3.1: The Pattern of Yggdrasill

WORKINGS

Continue with all your Daily Workings, including a form of the "Hammer-Working."

To this you will now add a more developed form of the "Yew-Working" which was started in the last Door. This working may be done separately from your daily routine— or it may be included within it.

The Yew-Working

The yew-rune (*ihwaz/eihwaz* ↓) describes the vertical dimension of the World-Tree, Yggdrasill. In it all the other vowel-runes U-A-I-E-O are contained.

The association of· a tree with the human psychosomatic complex (the complex of structures which make up the whole human being both *body* and *soul*) is well known in ancient Germanic religious conceptions. Humanity is shaped from "trees" by the gods Óðinn-Vili-Vé (see the *Gylfaginning* ch. 9 in the *Prose Edda*) or Óðinn-Hœnir-Lóðurr (see the "Völuspá" sts. 17-18 in the *Poetic Edda*). Both of these sets of divine triads are three-fold hypostases of Óðinn himself. Also, the sagas and *Eddas* abound with kennings which identify humans in terms of trees. It may indeed be said that humanity was shaped in the symbolic or spiritual image of the tree with aspects taking nourishment from the light and air of the heavens, and from the dark moisture of the Earth— all flowing and intermingling along the central trunk which synthesizes this polarity. It is in this context that the Yew-Working should be understood.

The Yew-Working seeks to synthesize the runic forces of the heavenly and chthonic streams in the consciousness of the Runer. It also serves to engage the consciousness of the Rune-worker into all the Rune- realms for more powerful *whole-concentration* and builds a foundation for full psychic integration with the complete runic cosmos of Yggdrasill.

The Yew-Working

(Preferably this working should be performed in bare feet on the surface of the earth.)

1. Stand with your arms at your sides facing north.

2. Settle and concentrate your mind with a few deep breaths (or you may conduct your breathing exercises from Door II at this point.

3. Center your attention below your feet, at the imaginary infinitely small center of the Earth, form where the subterranean streams of power spring— visualize this a pitch black and intone the formula **uuuuuuuuuuuu**— as this force rises from the center of the Earth and

streams into your feet where it is formulated into a black sphere of about 6″ diameter. At this point halt the intonation of the vocalic formula. Hold this image in your mind.

4. Turn your attention to the wide expanses of the World above your head. Visualize the zone of white energy of infinite expanse over your head while you intone the vocalic formula *aaaaaaaaaaaa* as this force flows from a wide expanse into a vertical column to the crown of your head, where a white sphere is formulated. Hold this image, along with that of the black sphere and stop for just a moment and consider the polarity between the two, and the force of attraction between them which is palpably manifested throughout the vertical column formed by the length of your body.

5. Next, turn your attention to the region of your genital organs and visualize a column of energy rising from the black sphere, slowly becoming a *deep blue* as it stops in the genital region and forms a deep blue sphere, as you intone the vocalic formula *iiiiiiiiiii*. Holding these various images, proceed to the next step.

6. Turn your attention to the region of your upper chest (at the top of your sternum) and visualize a column of force descending from the while sphere and the crown of your head, becoming pink and finally a *bright red* as it reaches your upper chest, where it too forms a bright red sphere. During this process, intone the vocalic formula *eeeeeeeeeeee*. Once this sphere has been established, you may halt the intonation of the formula and again pause and consider the polarity between these two complexes of cosmic energy. As you do so, you will feel the ever increasing force of attraction each has for the other.

7. Now visualize the forces of these two complexes simultaneously meeting in your solar plexus region where a bright green sphere is formed which radiates with a golden or bright yellow light from its center. Intone the vocalic formula *ooooooooooo* during this process. Concentrate on the wholeness of this structure and its fundamental unity with your*self*.

8. Now, to end the rite, begin to circulate the collected and intensified force from your center throughout the length of the structure with the vocalic formula *eeeeeeeeeeee* (a lax neutral vowel sound in which all of the muscles of the mouth are relaxed). The energy will flow up and down the length of the vertical column within your body, becoming focused and intensified at each of the centers, or wheels, within your system.

9. End by gathering all energy in the center and allowing it to re-balance itself throughout your system. Relax and finish with a few deep breaths.

Personal Analysis Diary III
(Life-Work)

At this point you have a complete runic analysis of your personality— at least at one level. These bright and murky lists should now be put into practice. In sections of the Third Door below, where you are asked to pick certain Runes to meditate on, etc.— use Runes that will either strengthen your bright characteristics or re-balance your weaknesses. This is especially valuable information you can utilize in such exercises as the runic breathing (below)— where the Rune is virtually absorbed into your very being in a highly intensified state.

Also, at this point the Runer should take up the intensive study of self-transformation. One of the best systems for our purposes is that of "psychosynthesis." The Runers may learn about all they need to know about this complex of techniques (of which they should make free use) in two books: *Psychosynthesis* and *the Act of Will* by Roberto Assaglioli. In addition, one might wish to start on the analysis of dreams. Probably the best system for this is provided by the *Jungian-Senoi Dreamwork Manual* by Stephon Kaplan Williams. Remember, the Odian explores many avenues— and not all Odians will make use of the same tools to grow. Generally we, as a culture, have placed too much importance on "dreams," which are most usually merely manifestations of our anxieties or wishes. Only rarely to the gods speak to us in dreams. Originally the Old English word *dream* referred to a reverie, a waking or *day*-dream. The Old English word for what we call a "dream" today is *swefen*— a nocturnal fantasy.

Vocalic Breathing III
(A)

By now in your general studies you should have a very good idea of the conceptual meanings behind each Runestave. Each stave should have a certain intuitive *feel* to it. This runic sense will continue to grow and deepen as you go deeper into Rune-thinking. However, at this point you can begin to make practical use of these senses.

A similar intuitive sense should now be cultivated for the "elements" (see *Futhark* pp. 74-75 and *Runelore* pp. 149-153). These "elements" are actually symbols for a certain virtually sensual categorization of subjective sensibilities. Use them in this way. You can intensify and re-balance your subjective universe through the use of these elemental symbols.

The Germanic System of Elements

The system of elements as taught within the traditional Germanic system is something different from that found within the Platonic-Hermetic tradition. Although the underlying principles are the same, and the methods of working with them is similar, they do represent two of the several different systems ultimately derived from the Indo-European system of the analysis of the subtle distinctions in substances.

In the Germanic system there are *two* primary elements:

FIRE, which is expansive heat and dynamic expansion, and **ICE**, which is contractive cold and absolute lack of vibration. In these two primary elements all absolute or extreme opposites are embodied: light and dark, energy and matter, etc. In addition there are two secondary elements derived from the primary ones: **AIR** (from **FIRE**) which is an all pervasive formless space, and **WATER** (from **ICE**) which is the still and deep matrix for form. In addition there are four lesser elements: **IRON** (inert hardness), **YEAST** (organicism), **SALT** (substance of organic life), and **VENOM** (dissolution). The final element, **EARTH**, is the synthesis of the other eight, and represents the ultimate state of potentialities.

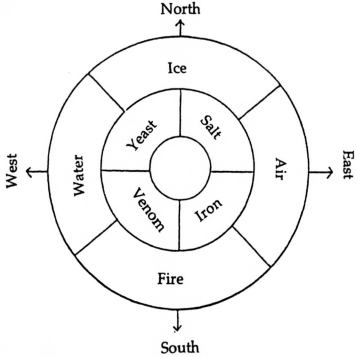

Figure 3.2: The Germanic System of Elements

Elemental Breathing

In a *staða* that is comfortable for you — sitting or standing — visualize yourself surrounded by a sphere. This sphere is filled with the essence of an *element* of your choice. Use whatever set of associations you need— color, smell, texture, and even sound or taste to evoke the essence of a given element. Fill the space of your sphere with it— make it intensely *present*. But the space that your body occupies within that sphere will be a vacuum with regard to that element. The essence is intense within the sphere— but totally lacking within your physical vehicle. Now, begin a regular rhythm of breathing. Visualize the essence of the element entering into the vacuum created by your body. With each breath you take more of the elemental essence within your personal space— and the intensity becomes correspondingly less within the sphere. Keep this up until you have totally reversed the polarity— now the element is intensely present in your body but it has been totally drawn out of the surrounding sphere. Do this a few times with each element.

(B)
Runic Breathing

There are a variety of techniques for runic breathing. Each of these methods should be experimented with.

(1) As above, you can fill a sphere surrounding your person (to a distance of some 4-5 feet around your body in all directions) with a certain runic force. Use Any keys— shape, color, etc., to evoke the presence of this force in the sphere. Remember to make your body-space void of this presence— it is the gap within a magical space. Again use a steady breath rhythm to draw all of the runic force out of the sphere into your personal space. It is now more completely brought under your control.

(2) Technique (1) is basically designed to be used with single Runes. However, you may also learn to "breathe the fuþark" by visualizing *fehu* before you and breathing it in (assimilating it into your lungs and spreading it throughout your system), then doing the same with *ūruz* and so on until you have gone through the whole fuþark. Especially in this exercise, but really with all similar work, it is good to concentrate on bringing in the force on the inhalation, on assimilating and distributing it throughout the system on the hold, and preparing the way for the next phase (Rune) on the exhalation— visualizing the next Rune during the out-hold phase of the rhythm.

(3) Another way to breathe the Runes is by breathing in the whole fuþark in one breath. This is best done with a slow rhythm. Visualize and audialize the Runes F through O being drawn in and circulated on the inhalation/hold and then reverse the process O through F upon exhalation— repeat as often as necessary. You can also do a similar

exercise in which the fuþark is divided into the airts (*ættir*)— and done eight at a time. Let your fetch be your guide.

BEGINNING GALDOR

The practice of galdor (OE *gealdor*, OHG *galster*, ON *galdr*) is the most effective magical combination of breath and sound— the incantation.

As most Runers already know, in the ancient North there were essentially two modes of magical workings differentiated by the Old Norse words *galdr* and *seið*. We will consider many details of *seið* in some detail in Doors VII-IX. For now, let it be said that *galdr* (galdor) is based on oral or vocalic performance and is rooted in verbal symbolism. The etymology of the word connects it with the word for the sound a crow or raven makes— *gala*, to call (as a raven). It might be further pointed out that the verbal/symbolic aspects of this kind of magic places it within the realm of Huginn (the left hemisphere of the brain). Conversely, the practice of *seidh* is within the realm of Muninn (the right hemisphere of the brain).

Practice

Actually, you have already made the first steps in the outer practice of galdor with the intonations of the vocalic sounds (in the yew-Working and in vocalic breathing). The true craft of galdor, however, is in the imbuing of the vibratory formulas with *meaning*, with traditional symbolic values that can then be used for magical (trans-formative) purposes. The book-tape package called *Rune-Song* from Rûna-Raven is perhaps your most easily available guide.

For the duration of this Door (240 days), practice and awaken each of the 24 staves for ten days in the following manner: Take the basic phonetic value, for example, ᚠ = [f] and combine it with the [ah]-sound (that is, of the A-rune. Repeat the resulting sound formula, in this instance [fah] in a monotonal song in which the f-sound and the a-sound are approximately of equal duration. Each singing of each combination should take up one exhalation of breath. When dealing with consonantal sounds that cannot be pronounced continuously, such as the k-sound, the short syllabic formula [ka] should be repeated until the breath is exhausted (**ka, ka, ka, ka, ka, ka**, etc.). The vowels can be combined (**a-u, a-a,** etc). With the A-rune you will be dealing with an essentially pure vocalic formula.

Now, as to the Runer's attitude during these exercises. The A-rune is used to awaken, and to keep awake certain levels of magical (Odian) consciousness. In this state of open awareness the symbolic values of the Runes can begin to be more deeply imbued into the sounds. The exact keys you use to activate these runo-symbolic values are somewhat left up to the individual Runer. But in general the esoteric key-words used in *Futhark*, *Runelore*, and *Runecaster's Handbook* might be your best guides. *Realize these* meanings as you sing the simple galdor formulas. You may supplement your exercises in any way you see fit with techniques of visualization you have learned already. Remember, you are helping to impress upon the sound-formula deep levels of meaning which you will later be able to call upon when needed. At first spend 5 minutes in this pursuit— extending it eventually to 10 minutes. This is a minimum time for regular practice.

Signing and Sending I

In *Futhark* (pp. 90; 133-135) the technique of sign-galdor was briefly mentioned. It is at this stage of Rune-Work that this practice will begin to be most beneficial. These pages in *Futhark* should be re-studied at this point. Some of the things expressed there may be more meaningful now than when you first read them.

This type of galdor is one that will continue to develop in the Runer almost indefinitely. The theory of how sign galdor works is a fascinating one. The outer technique of signing is simple. You merely trace the stave-form in the air before yourself with your finger, gand, or other suitable tool. (Of course, other signs and more complex *galdrastafir* are also executed in this fashion— but for now we are concentrating on the 24 Rune-staves.) The inner work which accompanies this outer performance is also fairly simple. Based on what you have learned and are learning about the energy system visualized in your body in the Yew-Working, you will have found the central column of power and the vertical epicenter of that column in the region of the "solar plexus." It is in this region — by means of the projecting instrument — that the Rune-sign will be cast forth to work your will.

Again, here you are to practice each of the 24 Rune-staves in succession for 10 days. Strongly visualize the stave flaming red in your "heart," (that is your ghostly heart or center wheel). When it is firmly fixed, either touch your center and with a sweeping gesture extend your arm straight out before you in preparation for tracing the stave, or simply visualize a beam of red or white light extending from your center to your already extended hand (as in Figure 3.3) The light is extended through your hand (and/or gand) forward to a point of your choosing in front of you. (A natural barrier, for example a wall or tree could be used; or you may wish to pick an imagined point in space before you for the manifestation of the signed stave.) At that point, trace the Rune-stave shape— you may also want to intone the Rune name at the same time, although you should also experiment in silence. During this phase, repeat the process — with full attention — from 10 to 20 times. You may do more if you find it effective.

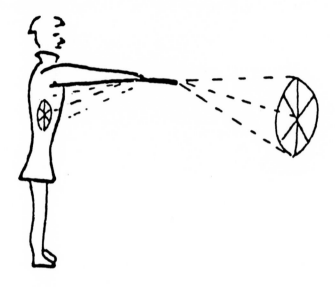

Figure 3.3: The Pattern of Signing and Sending

A brief word can be said concerning the symbolism of this technique.

Deep in our hearts all Runers carry the full matrix of Runestaves as a seed-form. This matrix can perhaps best be visualized as the seed-form **fuþark** as shown in Figure 3.4. Any one, or a combination of several, of these staves can be called out of this seed-form within the heart and made manifest within the subjective realm.

It will be noted that this seed-form or matrix (= Mother) Rune contains the shapes of all of the Runes of either the Elder or Younger **Fuþark** and that the form is not limited to a two-dimensional model. With imagination it can be seen in three as well as two dimensional form. Mediation on this matrix Rune will be in and of itself beneficial.

In the Armanen system of runology used by early 20th century rune-magicians, the HAGAL-rune (:✳:)was often said to be the "Mother-Rune," and it was under this influence that the text concerning it was written in the book *Futhark* (p. 36). it might be noted further that the HAGAL-based "Mother-Rune" seems to refer to a crystalline cube and to a mineral-based reality, whereas the figure below is a sort of helix, and reflects more of an organic reality. Ultimately, what is important to **realize** is that there is one *original* Rune from which all of the other Runes are derived.

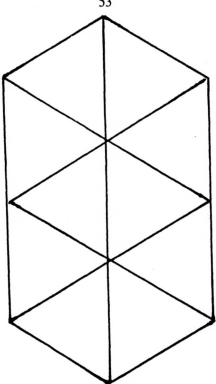

Figure 3.4: The Seed-Form Matrix of the Fuþark

In the heart the Rune is formed by the will of the Runer and given inner (subjective) life— it is then cast forth to the hand or gand (that is the active agent of the Runer's will) to effect changes in the objective world.

Through this tool of the will and image is shaped upon the objective world in accordance with that shaped in the subjective one— the Ring is being forged. The fact that the image cast upon the objective world is actually a shaping of the subjective world should not be lost!

Staða-Work III

For illustrations of the various stöður the Runer is referred to the Runic Tables in *Futhark*.

For 24 days, the Runer is to practice the I-rune staða. Begin with the 10 minutes attained in the standing position in the last Door, and expand it to 20 minutes by the end of the 24 day period. During this time you may intone the [i] vocalic formula and/or the Rune-name *isa*. Experiment with both possibilities— along with *silence*. Find out which of these variants helps you to call up the *significance* of *isa*. It might be interesting to note at this point that the early 20th century German runic occultists typically began their Rune-yoga exercises programs with the I-rune. (For more on this see *Rune-Might*, Llewellyn, 1989.) the main reason why it is used in this position here is its basic *simplicity* as a form, coupled with the cosmogonic fact that ice is the first material principle in Germanic cosmology— to which the first principle of energy — fire — is added...

Begin now with the F-rune and follow a similar plan as you did with the I-rune. Only this time you will practice for 18 days (not 24). Again, gradually increase your time of work from 5 to 10 minutes. Ten minutes is really a minimum time to aim for. On occasion you may feel called upon to go beyond this.

You will then proceed with the rest of the first half of the Fuþark (stave F - J), spending 18 days on each stave. This gives you 240 days for the completion of this Door. 24 (o) + 18 x 12 = 240.

Rune-Thinking III
(A)

Of course, much of the other work contained in this and previous Doors has been adding to your general skills of concentration and visualization. Here we will expand on the program of concentration and visualization, and bring that together with Rune-thinking. By now you have at least preliminarily meditated on 24 Runes of the Elder Fuþark and have gained a good deal of formal ability in concentrating on individual stave shapes. Over the 240 days of this Door, you should spend 10 days apiece on each of the 24 staves— imbuing them in silence with their esoteric meanings. In this phase — and aided by the other areas of work in this Door — you will charge or *load* the runic shape/name/sound with its hidden significances. You may use any method you wish to do this. One way is to associate freely concepts within the field of meaning attached to each stave while silently repeating the name of the Rune and strongly visualizing its shape. These concepts can be presented to the inner senses in many ways— for example as verbal concepts, as visual symbols, as sounds, even as smells, tastes, or tactile sensations. It all depends on what your mental "triggers" have been found to be. For example, with *fehu* one might use the verbal concepts: "money/power" (certainly still *loaded* words in modern English); the visual symbol might be stacks of greenbacks or ingots of gold; the sounds of the overture to *Das Rheingold*, etc. The point is to begin to build deep level associations between certain key ideas and the runic system. Each Rune should develop a "crystalline" sense for you— simple, perfect, beyond description in natural language.

In ancient times the Rune names themselves were so loaded with deep-level organic/cultural significance that the Runemasters probably had an easier time of it than we do today. If we seek deeply, however, we will find the loaded concepts in our own psyches that answer to the hidden inborn runic system.

Appendices to the Third Door
(A)
Basic Carving Techniques

In the next few Doors you will be concerned with the shaping of Rune-tines (or talismans) either for operative purposes or for divination. You should therefore begin to become familiar with various types of wood and the techniques the Runer employs in executing staves and other signs in wood.

It is commonly agreed that wood was the original medium into which Runestaves were executed. The runic technical terminology makes this quite clear. The most obvious example is the word "stave" (ON *stafr*; OHG *stab*; OE *stæf*) which literally just means stick or staff (of wood). The medium quickly became synonymous with the message (in this case), however, and soon the word "stave" took on all the connotations of "Rune." Even in later times when Runes and Rune-like signs were used in medieval and Reformation Age magical grimoires, the term used for "writing" these "staves" with pen and ink was related to the original word for "carving" or "cutting." This clearly shows that it is proper to use pen and ink in runic operations, but it is just as clearly demonstrated that the most traditional mode is that of carver (rister) and wood.

The tree and wood are, of course, very important in Germanic lore. Wood is the hard reliable — yet resilient and living — material which symbolizes the primary essence of humanity to which living consciousness was given by the divine triad of Wōðanaz-Wiljōn-Wīhaz. For this reason, in kennings humans are often paraphrased by tree names. It will be the task of the Runer to give to the already living essence of the wood a similar loading of *consciousness* and willed direction— be that for specific talismanic purposes of for the general shaping of Rune-lots for divination.

The archaeological record clearly shows various ways of carving Runes into a wide variety of media— wood, bone, metal and stone. A slightly different type of rister (carver) or sax (knife) is usually employed for the various media, but here we will concentrate on the rister or sax used to cut into wood.

One thing that is quite clear in the archaeological record, despite what you may have read, is that the Runestaves were almost always cut *across* or *against* (seldom with) the grain of the wood. That may be *one* reason why they generally avoid the 90-degree angle. This is done so that the lines of the Runestave will not get lost in the grain of the wood. When executed in this fashion the stave is clearly legible even without coloring.

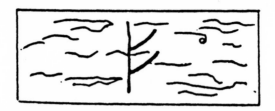

Figure 3.5: A Stave Carved Against the Grain

You should now set about practicing Rune-carving. Get a good supply of wood, and either with your rister of your sax, experiment with various methods of Rune-carving. You will see that you can easily, and quite quickly, scratch the Runes into the wood. This method is preferred if no color is to be added. But for more elaborate purposes you will want more smoothly and carefully to cut the Rune-shape out with the sharp blade of your sax. Really, the only limit placed on technique is the imagination and ability of the Runer— the archaeological record demonstrates this to us well.

Practice carving each of the 24 Runes. Then make a Runestave with all 24 Runes on it in the right order. Of course, the eventual aim is to be able to combine this technique with full magical attention/ visualization, so the more you can make this a concentrated exercise the better. But essentially at this point you are just getting familiar with your tools and the media.

(B)
Rune-Poems
During these 240 days, the Runer should memorize, if he or she has not done so already, the runic stanzas in English. At this point you may wish to memorize without using them directly in contemplation— that comes as you pass through the next Door.

The Old English Rune Poem
ᚠ (Wealth) is a comfort   to every man
although every man ought   to deal it out freely
if he wants, before the lord,   his lot of judgment.

ᚢ (Urox) is fearless   and greatly horned
a very fierce beast,   it fights with its horns,
a famous roamer of the moor it is a courageous animal.

ᚦ (Thorn) is very sharp;   for every thegn
who grasps it, it is harmful,   and exceedingly cruel
to every man   who lies upon it.

ᚠ (God) is the chieftain   of all speech,
the mainstay of wisdom   and comfort to the wise,
for every noble warrior   hope and happiness.

ᚱ (Riding) is in the hall   to every warrior
easy, but very hard   for the one who sits up
on a powerful horse   over miles of road.

ᚻ (Torch) is to every living person   known by its fire
it is clear and bright   it usually burns
when the noble-men   rest inside the hall.

ᚷ (Gift) is for every man   a pride and praise,
help and worthiness;   (and) of every homeless adventurer,
it is estate and substance for those who have nothing else.

ᚹ (Joy) is had   by the one who knows few troubles
pains or sorrows,   and to him who himself has
power and blessedness,   and also the plenty of towns.

ᚾ (Hail) is the whitest of grains, it comes from high in heaven.
a shower of wind hurls it,   then it turns to water.

ᚾ (Need) is constricting on the chest
although to the children of men it often becomes
a help and salvation nevertheless
if they head it in time.

ᛁ (Ice) is very cold   and exceedingly slippery;
it glistens, clear as glass,   very much like gems,
a floor made of frost   is fair to see.

ᛃ (Harvest) is the hope of men,   when god lets,
holy king of heaven,   the Earth give
her bright fruits to the nobles and the needy.

ᛇ (Yew) is on the outside   a rough tree
and hard, firm in the earth,   keeper of the fire,
supported by roots,   (it is a) joy on the estate.

ᛈ (Lotbox) is always   play and laughter
among bold men,   where the warriors sit
in the beer-hall,   happy together.

ᛨ (Elk's) sedge has its home   most often in the fen,
it waxes in the water   and grimly wounds
and burns with blood   any bairn
who in any way   tries to grasp it.

ᛋ (Sun) is by sea-men   always hoped for
when they fare away   over the fishes' bath (=sea)
until the brine-stallion (=ship)   they bring to land.

ᛏ (Tir) is a token,   it keeps troth well
with noble-men   always on its course
over the mists of night,   it never fails.

ᛒ (Birch) is without fruit   but just the same it bears
shoots without seed;   it has beautiful branches
high on its crown   it is finely covered
loaded with leaves,   touching the sky.

ᛗ (Horse) is, in front of the warriors,   the joy of noble-men,
a charger proud on its hoofs;   when concerning it, heroes—
wealthy men— on war-horses   exchange speech,
and it is to the restless   always a comfort.

ᛗ (Man) is in his mirth   dear to his kinsmen;
although each shall   depart from the other;
for the lord wants to commit,   by his decree,
that frail flesh   to the earth.

ᛚ (Water) is to people   seemingly unending
if they should venture out   on an unsteady ship,
and the sea-waves   frighten them very much,
and the brine-stallion   does not mind his bridle.

ᛝ (Ing) was first   among the East-Danes
seen by men   until he again eastward
went over the wave;   the wain followed on;
this is what the warriors   called the hero.

ᛞ (Day) is the lord's messenger,   dear to men,
the ruler's famous light;   (it is) mirth and hope
to rich and poor   (and) is useful to all.

ᚱ (Estate) is very dear   to every man,
if he can enjoy what is right   and according to custom
in his dwelling,   most often in prosperity.

ᚪ (Oak) is on the Earth   for the children of men
the nourishment of meat;   it often fares
over the gannet's bath (=sea):   The sea finds out
whether the oak keeps   noble troth.

ᚫ (Ash) is very tall,   (and) very dear to men
steady on its base,   it holds its stead rightly
though it is fought against   by many folks.

ᚣ (Bow) is for nobleman   and warrior alike
a joy and dignification,   it is excellent on a horse,
steadfast on an expedition—   (it is) a piece of war-gear.

ᛡ (Serpent) is a river-fish   although it always takes
food on land,   it has a fair abode
surrounded with water,   where it lives in happiness.

ᛏ (Grave) is hateful   to every warrior
when steadily   the flesh begins,
the corpse, to become cold,   to choose the earth
palely as a bed-mate;   fruits fall
joys pass away,   bonds of faith break.

The Old Norwegian Rune Rhyme

ᚠ (Gold) causes strife among kinsmen;
     the wolf grows up in the woods.

ᚢ (Slag) is from bad iron;
     oft runs the reindeer on the hard snow.

ᚦ (Thurs) causes the sickness of women;
     few are cheerful from misfortune.

ᚱ (Estuary) is the way of most journeys,
     but the sheath is (that way for) swords.

ᚱ (Riding), it is said, is the worst for horses;
  Reginn forged the best sword.

ᚢ (Sore) is the curse of children;
  grief makes a man pale.

ᚼ (Hail) is the coldest of grains;
  Christ shaped the world in ancient times.

ᚾ (Need) makes for a difficult situation;
  the naked freeze in the frost.

ᛁ (Ice), we call the broad bridge;
  the blind need to be led.

ᛅ (Harvest) is the profit of men;
  I say that Froði was generous.

ᛋ (Sun) is the light of the lands;
  I bow to the doom of holiness.

ᛏ (Týr) is the one-handed among the Æsir;
  the smith has to blow often.

ᛒ (Birch-twig) is the limb greenest with leaves;
  Loki brought the luck of deceit.

ᛘ (Man) is the increase of dust;
  mighty is the talon-span of the hawk.

ᛚ (Water) is (that), which falls from the mountain
  (as) a force; but gold (objects) are costly things.

ᛣ (Yew) is the greenest wood in the winter;
  there is usually, when it burns, singeing.

The Old Icelandic Rune Poem

ᚠ (Gold) is the strife of kinsmen   and fire of the flood-tide
          and the path of the serpent.
gold.   "Leader of the war-band."

ᚢ (Drizzle) is the weeping of clouds and the lessener of the rim of ice
    and (an object for) the herdsman's hate.
shadow, or shower   "Leader."

ᚦ (Þurs) is the torment of women   and the dweller in the rocks
    and the husband of the etin-wife Varð-rúna.
Saturn.   "Ruler of the legal assembly."

ᚨ (Ase) is the olden-father   and Asgard's chieftain
    and the leader of Valhalla.
Jupiter.   "Point-leader."

ᚱ (Riding) is a blessed sitting   and a swift journey
    and the toil of the horse.
journey.   "Worthy-man."

ᚲ (Sore) is the bale of children   and a scourge
    and the house of rotten flesh.
whip.   "King."

ᚻ (Hail) is a cold grain   and a shower of sleet
    and the sickness of snakes.
hail.   "Battle-leader."

ᚾ (Need) is the grief of the bondmaid   and a hard condition
    and toilsome work.
work.   "Descendant of the mist."

ᛁ (Ice) is the rind of the river   and the roof of the waves
    and a danger for fey men.
Ice.   "One who wears the boar helm."

ᛃ (Harvest) is the profit of all men   and a good summer
    and a ripened field.
Year.   "All-ruler."

ᛌ (Sun) is the shield of the clouds   and shining glory
    and the life-long sorrow of ice.
Wheel.   "Descendant of the victorious one."

ᛏ (Týr) is the one-handed god   and the leavings of the wolf
       and the ruler of the temple.
Mars.   "Director."

ᛒ (Birch-twig) is a leafy limb   and a little tree
       and a youthful wood.
Silver fir.   "Protector."

ᛘ (Man) is the joy of man   and the increase of dust
       and the adornment of ships.
Human.   "Generous one."

ᛚ (Water) is a churning lake   and a wide kettle
       and the land of fish.
Lake.   "Praise-worthy one."

ᛇ (Yew) is a strung bow   and brittle iron
       and a giant of the arrow.
Bow.   "Descendant of Yngvi."

      *   *   *   *   *

These poems along with the texts in the original languages read on tape by the Yrmin-Drighten are available on the *Rune-Song* tape from Rûna-Raven. A more scholarly and complete presentation of the entire corpus of the rune poems, with a glossary of the old languages is contained in the volume *The Rune-Poems I*.

(C)
Basic Runecasting: History and Theory

The practice of runic divination is certainly an ancient one. All evidence points to this being one of the original uses of the Runestaves. If, in theory, Rune galdor is the *active* sending of the will and consciousness of the Runer into his objective environment or subjective reality (thus altering it), then conversely the practice of runic divination is the passive reception of impressions from either the objective environment or from otherwise hidden aspects of the subjective reality. This is divination in the truest sense.

The whole technical vocabulary of Runelore points to the original use of Rune*staves* for divinatory purposes. Unfortunately, *none* of the actual "blood-twigs" has survived in the archaeological record. This may not be so surprising, however, if we consider that they were usually made of wood and surely have decayed by now, and that such Runestaves were sometimes willfully destroyed after they had fulfilled their purposes anyway.

Of course, the oldest account of runic divination is perhaps to be found in chapter 10 of the *Germania* of Tacitus. The ritual formula depicted there is the simplest one still in use among Runers. The *Poetic Edda* also contains cryptic lines that obviously refer to an elaborate divinatory practice, for example in the "Völuspá" st. 20 and "Hávamál" sts. 80 and 111. We also have a number of accounts in which the casting of lots (presumably marked with Runes) was used to decide legal cases (in the *Frisian Laws*) to decide the propriety of sacrifice (in *The Life of St. Willibrordi*) or to select war leaders (in Bede's *History of the English Church*).

Theories as to how divination of all sorts is supposed to work abound in occult literature and lore. These explanations range from no theory at all — pure belief in the "inherent magic" of the Tarot cards, lines on the hand, etc., — to sophisticated ideas on synchronicity. For the true Odian the ultimate explanation as to how Runecasting (or Runecraft) works is not to be found in theories or in the belief in inherent powers of the arrangement of certain lines— but rather it is to be found in the *self* of the Runer. To a certain limited degree Runelore is valid for those who blindly believe and for those who see the Runes as arbitrary signs and who think the Roman or Hebrew alphabet would serve just as well. But it works in a whole new dimension for those who have given themselves to themselves and who have learned to impress upon these fertile shapes the seed concepts born within the will and inner sight that they may grow with a might greater than any previously conceived.

In more general writings I have usually given more "traditional" explanations of things— which only hinted at the more esoteric practical truth lying just behind the tradition. Now, in the middle of this systematic initiation into the secrets of truly hidden lore you will want to delve beyond the outer tradition into the inner workings. You have, if you have been faithfully working, started this and are by now at a fairly advanced level.

At this point you should review "The Theory of Rune-Galdor" in Door II if you are not thoroughly familiar with the ideas contained in those pages. It will be clear to those who are, that the first step in effective Runecraft of any sort is the loading of the Runestaves with associations and then using those Runestaves as symbols of those meanings in a form of communication with various aspects of the world. This is analogous to the way a child learns words, connects them to ideas/things and then learns to understand them when heard (and eventually read) and to use them in active speech (and eventually in writing). This takes place in a progressively more complex system of contexts. The child learns to comprehend and express ever more complex messages, and perhaps to imbue those messages with deeper layers of meaning. We are faced with a similar situation with the Runes.

On one level, in Runecasting the Runer hears the direct voice of the god within — but less poetically the Runer receives messages from the objective or subjective realities in a language that he or she has both learned (from tradition) and thought (within the context of the subjective/objective universes). The *objective* validity of the Runes as a "language" for this exchange of meaningful communications lies in two factors: 1) they are *traditional* (the symbolic associations have a long and valid history and were handed down for centuries in unaltered or systematically evolved forms), and 2) they are metagenetic and meta-linguistic (for persons of Germanic heritage they are *your* esoteric tradition, and for all native English speakers they have their roots in your *very linguistic structure*). It is these factors that make the tradition-al Runestaves and the runic system a potent foundation for the workings of the Odian consciousness.

Once you have "learned the inner language" of the Runes, you are ready to engage in true initiated runic divination— not "playing" at Runes.

Given the cosmo-psychological context, the actual way in which runic divination works is simple. Every method of Runecasting will consist of two elements: 1) the *Runestaves* (in our communication model the equivalent of the "words" in natural language), and 2) a *stead* or predetermined meaningful position in which a Runestave may or may not find itself cast or laid (the equivalent of a syntactic position or part of speech in a sentence). In order to make the Runes truly speak to you, you must follow a certain inner procedure. First a link must be forged between the subjective and objective universes — your inner Yggdrasill is linked with the World-Yggdrasill — to establish a full range of communicative possibilities. Second, a specific question is posed within this linked context. Concentration at this stage is most important because there the actual inner question is being sent to the linked context. A lack of concentration will send "mixed signals" and result in a less reliable reading. Third, the Runecast is made in this state— at which point the link is broken. The return message has been sent and now it is up to the Runer to interpret the message. The fourth step is the actual "reading of the Runes." This is an *active* not a *passive* endeavor. The passive aspect is only present in the time while the link is in effect. Therefore the actual Rune-reading is a synthesis of the active and passive functions— as is the interpretation of mundane language. This whole inner and outer process is what is meant by "learning to read the Runes aright."

For the non-Odian, such a process will be perceived as one in which the Runer poses a question to the objective universe — or to objective entities within it (for example, the norns [note small "n"]) — who then manipulate the Runestaves as they are in a randomized chaotic state (for example, as they are in the air falling to their steads on the white cloth).

But for the true Odian who has learned to expand his consciousness into the objective "other" universe symbolized by the nornic entities — who has learned to give his eye to Mímir's Well — a more direct and independent course is indicated. For a time, the Runer may find himself on a road between these two understandings.

The Fourth Door of Midgard

— Opening —

With the completion of the *Fourth Door* the Runer will have completed the great work of preparation for full initiation into the Runes. By the end of this *Door* the meditative work will be finished, and more concentration will be placed in future Doors on working with the Runes as you have been able to *internalize* them. Of course, the process of absorbing and learning the Runes is, and should remain, a never-ending one. You should return regularly to basic Rune-thinking in order to *re-load* your battery, so-to-speak. Quantitative as well as qualitative benefits are to be derived from such review practice. But it is also true that such a review will be an ongoing process in the Rune-work ahead.

Reading

Suggested readings for the Fourth Door:
Myths and Symbols of Pagan Europe, H.R. Ellis Davidson
Egil's Saga, Snorri Sturluson
In Search of the Indo-Europeans, J. P. Mallory
A History of the Vikings, Gwen Jones
The Birth of the Middle Ages 395-814, H. St. L.B. Moss
The Germanization of Early Medieval Christianity, James Russell.
Rune-Magic, Siegfried Adolf Kummer

WORKINGS

Here you are to continue with the regular discipline of the Daily Work and continue to develop the Yew-Work. However, you should also now institute a special *staða*-working just before beginning the Yew-Work. This *staða*-working will prepare you quite well for the more complex *staða* experiments in the tradition of the twentieth century Rune-magicians Friedrich Bernhard Marby, Siegfried Adolf Kummer, and Karl Spiesberger which will follow in coming Doors. (This magical technique is also covered in detail in my book *Rune-Might*.)

Loading *Staða*-Work

This is designed to bring the Runer into a relaxed and balanced state fully loaded with potential expressions of Rune-might. This sequence is used by the German magicians as a formula of engagement.

Facing north, with a regular breathing pattern, perform the three Rune-*stöður* ᛁ - ᚢ - ᛉ while singing the Rune-name of each in sequence. You may repeat the sequence several times— especially in the beginning. Bring as much of the Rune-meaning into your consciousness as possible while performing the *staða*. Normally one *staða* per breath-cycle is executed. However, you may also experiment with moving quickly but smoothly from one *staða* to the next through the row of three on one breath-cycle. The aim of the working is to feel the influx of Rune-might— which comes from a centered stable ego-being (*ek*) = I — drawing from below telluric forces to strengthen the will = ᚾ — and drawing from above on the archetypal forces of divine consciousness along the Bifröst-Bridge = ᛦ.

Now move on to the expanded Yew-Work.

Yew-Work III

(A)

This initial exercise will last 120 days. In order to intensify the power of the Yew-column — or Irminsūl — you are now to add definite runic significances to the vertical columns of light which connect the five spheres of the internal Yew. (See Figure 4.1)

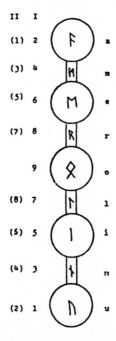

Figure 4.1: The Runic Yew-column

Now, for example, instead of moving from the a-sphere to the i-sphere (as in program I), attention should be more directly focused on the column rising through the legs toward the genitals in the i-sphere. In this column intone the n-sound (or the Rune name *nauþiz*). It will give a spinning sensation in that region of the body (especially in the knees) as if the need-fire were being kindled on the top of the u-sphere by a boring action of the column of light. When the m-column is called upon, you should feel a gentle tugging sensation through your head as if something were being pulled into your being from the outside and above your whole cranium (in a sort of funnel shape). Once the two upper and lower dyads [ᚠ-ᛗ-ᛗ] and [ᚢ-ᛏ-ᛁ] have been established, there will be a qualitative difference in the activation of the l- and r-columns and the o-sphere. With the l-column, visualize a seething morass of unformed life energy in the region of your belly while intoning the l-sound— now quickly in conjunction with this visualize in the heart region a descending conical spiral of fiery energy while intoning the r-sound. These two forces meet at a point in a clap of thunder and a flash of lightning and sparks fly. (See Figure 4.2.)

Figure 4.2: The Meeting of the Upper and Lower Columns

From that meeting point the o-sphere arises and expands. At this moment the o-sound is then intoned to activate fully the o-sphere in its balanced dynamic state.

As you see in this working process the Runer re-creates a process similar to, but not identical to, the cosmogonic myth in his being daily. This pattern of energy alternating between poles rather than a straight line of manifestation is a unique and powerful feature of the magical Germanic world-view. Therefore, you should work this pattern at least through the time of this Door. In the future the Runer will be more free to experiment with linear patterns.

However, you are encouraged to alternate regularly between the two sequences of development I and II (as indicated in Figure 4.1) it has been found that some Runers respond better when beginning with ᚠ- (Asgard), while others do better beginning with ᚻ- (Hel). In fact, these are simultaneous, or synchronic. As your levels of visualization and concentration rise, you will even be able to call upon both poles at the same time and recreate the process more precisely. Although vocal performance will be limited.

Yew-Work III
(B)
120 Days

After performing the complete manifestation of the vertical column for 120 days, a new phase is to be entered upon which will fulfill the entire Yggdrasill pattern in the physical being of the Runer. Perform the Yew-Work as before, only now as the forces of the r- and l-columns meet, direct the lightning bolts to the four cardinal points at the border of your personal sphere. These will be directed to points in front of and behind you, and to your left and right at 3-4 feet away from your center. At these points activate four spheres equal in size to your internal spheres (wheels).* Before you is the icy sphere of Niflheimr, behind you the fiery sphere of Muspellsheimr, to your right and left the shining spheres of Jötunheimr and Vanaheimr respectively. Strongly establish the presence of these four spheres in shining radiance— each powerfully pulsing with vital energy. Use the sound of the F-rune is doing this. You will notice that you are strengthening already established patterns, as the spheres will be at those points occupied by the hammers (or Runes) from the Hammer-Work (or the runic equivalent). The beams connecting the Runer's center with these outer points should also be strengthened in this phase. After some time (about 9 breaths), with the four outer spheres firmly fixed, activate the central o-wheel (with the o-sound). In activating it, you should be aware of its being fed from all four lateral spheres (through the horizontal beams) and from above and below on the Yew-column. Now circulate the vertical and horizontal forces, visualizing force going up and down the vertical column and circulating around the four outer realms in a clockwise direction. Remain in this state for at least five minutes, and experiment with longer periods.

---

* These are called "wheels," Old Norse *hvél*, which answers to the Sanskrit word for "wheel," *ćakra*. As the body is seen as a vehicle, the "wheels" are the means by which dynamic movement is effected. This image certainly goes back to Indo-European times when folks first moved about on the steppes in wheeled wagons.

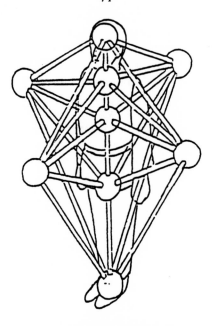

Figure 4.3: The Complete Establishment of Yggdrasill
in the Personal Sphere

Advanced Breath Techniques

The Runer will want to continue using the very basic forms of runic breathing given in the last Door throughout this or her work at various times. The discipline of Rune-singing or galdor imposes its own form of breath training as well. But there is a form of breath-work which treats breath (or air/wind) as a source of power in its own right. In our tradition it is called *önd* in Old Norse, or *æþm* in Old English. Nowadays we can call it athem. The root of the word *æþm* is related to the Sanskrit *ātman*, breath and soul— which eventually becomes a word for Self. In the Indo-European system (from which the Germanic and Indic systems were both derived) we know that breath was considered a source of *spiritual* power and that this was a special aspect of the tripartite gift of Wōðanaz-Wiljōn-Wīhaz. In the Old Norse tradition the *önd* is the particular gift of Óðinn himself (Völuspá 18). Athem, or *önd*, is the source of pure undifferentiated energy which is regularly circulated in the human being through breathing. The control of this process therefore would be analogous to controlling energy supply within the psychosomatic complex. Of course, our Indian brothers have developed this aspect to a science, a discipline called *pranayama*. Perhaps the best general treatment of this practice is provided by Andre van Lysebeth (*Pranayama: the Yoga of Breathing*. London: Unwin, 1979). This book has the advantage of having been written by a "westerner" while at the same time being quite traditional in its approach. Other books on *pranayama* could also be used to get the details of this practice. But in all cases, two things must be kept in mind: 1) these seemingly "eastern" practices have an ultimately Indo-European origin and actually represent sophisticated developments of basic magico-shamanistic techniques, and 2) you may feel free to "runicize" the various symbol systems used in these practices. An opportunity to provide an example of how to do this is given on p. 127 of the van Lysebeth book. There we read of the practice of the *samavritti pranayama* or "pranayama square." This could be converted to a runic formula thusly:

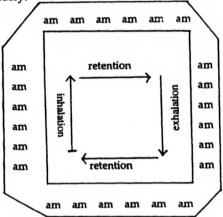

This method allows the Runer to count six seconds or beats of the heart (one for each uttering of the syllable *am*) and thereby ensuring a regular rhythm without *counting* by means of profane numbers. It should be noted that the syllable *am* relates to the region of the head, being the sounds of the transpersonal intelligence *ansuz* combined with the manifestation of that intelligence in *mannaz*. (See the Yew-Working for further insights.) Also, with regard to this formula: it is very much akin to the Indian formula *om*. (See Mircea Eliade's book *Yoga* for some no-nonsense views on this sacred syllable.) For us, it represents the minimal expression of the full range of vowel sounds. An extended version of this formula would be "aueiom" or "aoueim." these phonically represent the sense of entirety and a projection of magical essence and power from the depths of being (symbolized by the back of the throat) into outer manifestation (the closed lips).

Galdor II

After having practiced each of the 24 Runes individually and in their simplest forms, you are now ready to realize fully the power of intoning the Rune-names and the more complete *galdrar* given in *Futhark* or on the tape *Rune-Song*. Over the 240 days of this Door you should practice as follows. Intone the name of the Rune nine times—slowly. Then combine each sound with the five main vowel sounds. So, *fehu* would sound like this:

fehu fehu fehu / fehu fehu fehu / fehu fehu fehu
fa / fu / fe / fi / fo

In this system of notation, the slashes represent breaths. Remember to practice breath control here as in all other types of work. One secret to effectiveness in such work is the concentration of attention in the various wheels within the body (see the Yew-Work) as the corresponding vowel sound is intoned. (This is true for Rune names, the abstract vocalic formulas, or any other vocal work. Ten days should be spent on each stave.

Once the general principles of this kind of work have been grasped, the Runer will begin to want to shape galdor to his or her own special ends. Through a combination of symbolically significant consonantal and vocalic runic sounds the Runer will be able to *speak the language of the gods*. The principles taught here are also to be taken into account when reciting poetic (skaldic) words in a working setting. Great power will flow forth from one who speaks the skaldic tongue with full might and mind! In the following Doors various galdor practices and workings will be suggested— but the mainstays should already be clear.

Signing and Sending II

Now that the general technique of signing and sending Runes has been established, it is time to use this technique in a more operative way. The Runer should now employ the full technique of signing the Runes and holy signs in the performance of a *sphere working* such as that described in *Futhark* (pp. 91-93) under the "Hammer Rite." For the Runer a special runic form of this working should be employed — the Hail Working. This is best done just following the Yew Working. The ultimate aim of this combination of workings is the construction of an operative sphere fully arrayed with the Runes in the objectified walls of the sphere and fully alive in the subjective Tree of Yggdrasill within the sphere. This includes the Yew-column down the vertical center of the Runer. The building of this operative body is one of the greatest Runes of the Gild.

The internal side of this body has already begun to be substantially built up in your Yew Work; now we want to build a stronger sphere surface. This can be done by means of the Hail-Work. Remember, the sphere wall is not an iron plate to protect you from anything, but rather a willfully imposed borderland between the objective and subjective worlds and a means of filtering and selecting influences— both incoming and out-going. It is a sort of semipermeable membrane.

Hail-Work

1) Face the North-Star

2) Beginning with *fehu* in the north, sign and send the Runes of the fuþark in a ring around you at the level of the solar plexus at about 4-5 feet out in front of you. Here, turn "with the sun" (in a clockwise direction), signing and sending each of the Runestaves— tracing them about a foot in length in red light while intoning their names— until all 24 have been completed and the ring is closed in the north with *ōþala* next to *fehu*.

3) Stand in the cross-*staða* and visualize an equilateral cross lying horizontally in the plane of the Rune ring and your solar plexus, with that point as the center of the cross. The arms of the cross should end at the points where they intersect the Rune band. Imagine a surrounding band of shimmering blue light with the red Rune band as its equator. Then visualize the vertical axis coming through your length from the infinite space above and from the infinite space below.

4) Feel and see the force flowing into your center from all six directions in beams of blue light.

5) Sign and send a shining blue *hagalaz*-rune (either in the h or h forms) to a place just on the inside wall of the sphere superimposed over the *fehu*-rune about two feet in length. Intone the words *hagala wīh-hailagaz* (o hail [make] sacro-sanct!). Turning widdershins (counter clockwise) repeat this formula in the west, south, and east.

Returning to the north, direct your attention to the floor of the sphere and repeat the *hagal*-formula, and then do the dame overhead. As you sign the *hagalaz*-runes below and above, visualize their arms extending in such a way as to make contact with the ones on the plane from an external web-work of blue beams over the surface of the sphere.

6) In the cross-*staða* again intone *hagala wīh-hailagaz*! Strongly visualize the full array of the red Runes and the web-work of blue *hagalaz* Runes.

The Hail-Work forms a potent working atmosphere— especially when combined with the Yew-Work, but as far as the particular technique of signing and sending is concerned it also gives an added dimension. Once you are able to establish this complex body of light firmly, and you wish to sign and send, let us say the might of *kēnaz* (to increase creative powers), then you would simply turn to that Runestave in the Rune-ring and sign and send (in a steady stream of force) the Rune through that portion of the Rune-ring. To aid in such an operative working, you could set up a symbol of the person or thing to the affected at a position just outside the sphere at the point of the relevant Rune-stave so that the force flow would be seen to come from your center through the Rune to the object of the working. For subjective workings (that is, working on changes within the self) the Runer can draw power through one Rune or a combination of Runes in conjunction with *önd*-work (breathing exercises).

Staða-Work IV

Here the Runer should simply continue with the *staða*-working of the staves ᚾ through ᛉ as outlined in *Futhark*, and as discussed in the previous Door. Spend 18 days on each stave, and end the series as you began with 24 days of the *isa*-rune. This makes a total of 240 days for this Door.

Now, the practice of the *stöður* will be taking on added power as you increase the potency of the working atmosphere within your personal ring. It will be learned how the *stöður* are truly activation of the space within the sphere in conjunction with the Yew-column (and branches) and the Rune-ring. The secrets of the methods by which *staða*-work actually has its effect are now being shown to you— by experience, not by dogma.

Rune-Thinking IV

Now that the Rune-staves have been loaded with their seed-principles, it is time to expand them fully and in a traditional manner by contemplation of the ancient Rune-poem stanzas in conjunction with the stave shape, and other attributes.

As a schedule, you will spend four days apiece on the 28 stanzas of the Old English Rune Poem, four days apiece on the 16 stanzas of the Old Norwegian Rune Rhyme, and four days apiece of the 16 stanzas of the Old Icelandic Rune Poem. This makes a total of 240 days of poetic contemplation.

The method is as follows. Call up the hidden meanings of the Rune-stave through a nine-fold calling of its name. Once the "feel" of the Rune has been established recite (silently or aloud) from the heart the relevant Rune poem stanza. Now, dwell upon the complex meaning and allow your thoughts to roam freely. Seek out hidden links, first within the stanza, then within the whole of the Rune poem in question, then within the whole of the runic tradition or system. This includes the sounds, shapes, order, names, meanings, and any other associations. At the conclusion of each of these sessions write down your results. Also, do not be surprised if at various times during the day further realizations based on your contemplations are found. Be prepared to record these as well.

One note on the Old English system is in order. Because of the extension of the Anglo-Frisian system from 24 to 28 (and eventually to 33) Runes there will be some staves in the Old English Rune Poem contemplation which you have perhaps not considered previously. Here, the book *Rune-Games* by Marijane Osborn and Stella Longland will be of great use. A main task of the Runer will be to see how certain aspects of the esoteric lore of the Elder Fuþark were extracted by early Ingvaeonic Runemasters and applied to the expansion of the runic system. See if there is anything genuinely new or different in these extra Runes to be conveyed to the specifically Anglo-Frisian mind.

Also, you are encouraged to continue with the type of very basic runic meditations suggested in Door III.

Taufr I

Basic practical work concerning the planning and construction of runic talismans or "Rune-tines" is covered in *Futhark* pp. 98-124.

The practice of *taufr* is the best documented form of ancient Rune galdor. This is because we have, in the form of runic inscriptions, the outermost form of *taufr*, and because it is the type of Rune galdor most often mentioned and explained in the Old Norse literary sources. In its simplest form, *taufr* consists of a threefold process of risting, reddening and rowning, that is of carving, coloring and charging the formula. Extremely simple forms of *taufr* will only be effective when performed by fairly advanced Runers— most will want to make use of various ritual formulas to help in the overall process of concentrating and directing the will to do its work. The most usual form of *taufr* (magic) does not involve the invocation of any "magical agent" outside the Runer. The point of *taufr* is to influence the objective (or subjective) world directly by means of the will— and to shape a creature out of your own essence to carry out this will.

Even though a fairly complete outline of *taufr* is given in *Futhark*, the material given here will teach certain secrets beyond those discussed there.

As an exercise in basic *taufr* — which will also be of direct benefit to the work of this Door — the Runer should set about shaping Rune-tines for the work of Runecasting. Plan to shape one tine per day. This could be made part of your regular sessions, or you could make this the subject of special workings. The form of the tines could be traditional staves (twigs or elongated strips of wood about 6″ long and 1/4-1/2″ across), or flat card-like slips of wood (about 1/2-1″ wide and 1-2″ long). Either form, or other forms, as discussed in *Runecaster's Handbook* (pp. 67-70), may be used in any kind of Runecasting or Rune-laying operation. You may select any kind of wood for these workings, but oak, ash or yew, or any fruit-bearing tree or bush (that is, those with edible berries or nuts) would be preferred.

The actual construction working is simple. In the right operative atmosphere (if you are not doing this as a part of your regular session you will want to build the "ghostly hall" of the Rune-ring and sphere around yourself), take the raw tine and point it toward all eight "horns of heaven." (That is, point it in all eight compass directions.) Now, facing north, sit down and carve the Rune into the stave— continuously singing the Rune name or the more expanded galdor. Concentrate all that you know of the Rune into your work— feel and see that meaning flow from your heart into the Rune-shape. Now color the Rune with red pigment or with blood, while concentrating in a similar manner. Once you have finished doing all 24 tines, store the Rune-tines in a special location, for example wrapped in a black cloth in a box. These tines will be of use to you in operative as well as illuminative work.

Taufr-Work

The ritual instructions given in *Futhark* represent the most complete and elaborate type of taufr ritual practiced by the Gild. As experience is gained, the Runer will learn to do with less and less ceremonial as he or she learns to impress the will more and more directly into the objective or subjective universal web-works.

Quite ironically, one of the secret ways in which the Gild practices *taufr* is to state explicitly yet poetically the aims of the working in natural language. This great "secret" is ironic because this is precisely the form most often used by the elder generation of Runers, and therefore should be obvious to the modern generation— yet often is not.

To formulate and execute *taufr* of this kind the Runer must be familiar with a vast body of lore. This lore comes from essentially two sources: 1) the mythology and 2) the language to be used. The former may not be useful in all workings, but the latter is always essential. Now your work in skald-craft is to begin.

To be able to formulate effective *formálar* one must have a basic word-hoard made up of Germanic roots words (that is modern English words of Germanic origin) and a way of putting them together that is magically effective— that is *poetic*. The greatest exemplary guide in this pursuit is Lee Hollander's translation of *The Poetic Edda*. (See also Appendix C, p. 142 in *Futhark*.) You may make your poetic forms as elaborate as your abilities allow, but you should always remember that the poetics, like the use fo numerical symbolism, is usually an *intensifier* of the message and not the message itself. The form of the message makes it more effective, but it is the substance of the will carried by the forms that actually does the work. In other words, never compromise the substance to the outer form.

In order to establish a basic vocabulary from which to work, you should sit down with a good dictionary (one with etymologies) and make lists of all words of Germanic origin (especially Old English [Anglo-Saxon] and Old Norse)— but also words of Celtic origin which seem compatible could be added. Such lists should be arranged acrophonically, that is according to initial sound and in the fuþark order. After you have gone through the dictionary (by the way the *Oxford English Dictionary* is ideal for this) you will have what amounts to a "rhyming dictionary" for alliterative modern Germanic poetry.

Now, how should such a list be used in formulating effective verse? The simplest guidelines are as follows: The basic formal aspect of Germanic verse is alliteration or "stave-rhyme," and the half-line, You should aim to have three stave rhymes per whole line (that is two half-lines put together). Try to keep the syllable count even from one whole-line to the next. Also, it is usually more euphonious in modern English if the alliterating staves are separated from one another by intervening words— otherwise it starts to sound like "Peter Piper picked..." In the rules of alliteration all vowels alliterate will each other. Another great guiding principle is economy. Never use more words than you really need to state your magical message.

These basic guidelines are really all the Runer needs to begin to compose effective skald-craft.

An example of such a formula for the gaining and keeping of monetary wealth could be:

:ᚠ: ᚠ:ᛁ·ᚠᚱᚢᚾᛏᛗ:ᚠᛏᛗ·ᚺᛗᛚᛗ·ᛁᛏ·ᚠᚠᛋᛏ:

A f(ee) I found   and held it fast

Note: Four syllables to each half-line, three stave-rhymes on f (=underlying Rune-might being channeled), Rune-count = 21 = 1 (quite compatible with the aim of the working). Also note that the verb tenses are in the past. This is "symbolic" of the action having taken place in reality, and to be a part of the objective universe already.

Runecasting II

Runecasting is, of course, fully covered in *Runecaster's Handbook.* That text should be used as a sort of basic textbook for what will be said here. Now is the time to take up the study of Runecasting in an in-depth way.

The Ritual of Runecasting

In the process of learning the "feel" of interpreting Runes in given Runecasting systems the Runer will often want to make "hypothetical castings," that is ones that may or may not be highly significant. However, when a serious inquiry is to be made, it should not be taken lightly. One must "ask the Runes aright" before they can be "truly tried and trusted to rown right rede." In order to ensure the proper framework for such a casting, a traditional ritual setting must be established. This signals the runic realms within the self that a full and whole link is made between the objective and subjective worlds. Now the Rune-rede will be more effective and trustworthy.

In the ritual below we have basically given two forms (A) for the casting method and (B) for the lay-out method of actually establishing runic data. Experiment with both forms.

The Work of Runecasting

1) Raise the Rune-hall (runic sphere) about yourself.

2) Still facing north, lay before you, in the center of the room, the white cloth (at least 3' x 3' in size), with the words:

"World all-wide, I shall read the Rune aright!"

[This establishes the objective field into which the Runes will be cast and read— or projected and analyzed.]

3) In the Y-*staða* and with your eyes uplifted (if performed out of doors gaze upon the Northern Star)— call upon the three-fold Nornic force with the words:

"Wend forth out' the wide worlds
ye maidens all-mighty
out' the eastern darkness enter
— Urðr - Verðandi - Skuld —
a. within you I strew the staves!
or
b. within you I lay the lots!

4) Holding the Runestaves in your hands before you with your head again uplifted— silently and intently concentrate upon the question or situation of concern. You may also sing, silently or aloud, the names "Urðr-Verðandi-Skuld." Once the link has been made, end this part with the words:

"Runes rown right rede!"

(*Rúnar ráða rétt ráð!*)

[This establishes a link between the precise form of your question and the gathered processes and "Nornic forces."]

5) Either (A) cast the staves out before you in a random manner (do not take your eyes away from their northerly gaze) or (B) sit down before the cloth and randomly choose the right number of staves from the bundle in your hands and lay them out in the predetermined pattern (see below). In either case, again sing he Nornic names— "Urðr - Verðandi - Skuld" as you cast or lay out the Runes.

6) (A) With your eyes closed or still focused upward and northward, kneel down and feel your way across the cloth with your left hand and pick up the right number of staves at random. Pass each one into your right hand one at a time and place each in its proper stead for interpretation (see below). Once the choosing is complete, gaze down upon the Runes and read them aright.

(B) You now have the proper lay-out before you, gaze upon the Runes and read them aright.

[Ultimately, in both forms you will be faced with similar runic data as described below. You may take as long to interpret these data as necessary.]

7) After interpreting (reading) the Runes, make a record of the lay-out in a notebook prepared for this purpose. Many significant readings will

not be realized until perhaps later — in a flash of insight, or perhaps during later workings — so it is important to keep records of all castings. Now, silently and solemnly return the staves to their place of storage (in their box or cloth bag) and perform the customary closing working.

8) You may now wish to elaborate on your record of the casting— write a detailed interpretation, etc. Objectifying the reading in this way is most valuable. It prevents the tendency for Rune-readings to shift about in the subjective universe and become distorted. You may alter your reading later— based on new insights or increased knowledge — but at least have a definite reading to work off of.

9) Right after the conclusion of especially important castings, the Runer will want to take "hail-signs" (ON *heilar*, omens). This particular feature of Germanic divination is discussed at length below.

The Practice of Rune-Reading

There are a great number of methods of Rune-casting or Rune-laying, all of which basically work on the juxtaposition of the Runes (with more or less stable meanings) with predetermined steads (with various significances). The reading is a synthesis from elements among the Rune, the stead, and the mind of the Runer. More advanced and perhaps more precise forms of runecasting are part of the teachings of the Rune-Gild.

<u>Rune Meanings</u>

The meanings of each Rune-stave could be intuited from information given in already published works. But for specific divinatory purposes, the following tables are offered to the Runer. All Runers should keep a notebook in which definite expansions on these meanings which have been intuited by the Runer are recorded so that they can be employed in future castings.

Here the positive readings of the Runes are followed by the negative manifestations of the same mystery.

Runic Tables

ᚠ   New beginning, social success, foresight, energy, travel, money, control; or greed, failure, atrophy, poverty, discord.

ᚢ   Strength, constancy, vitality, tenacity, pattern, luck, health, knowledge, understanding; or weakness, obsession, misdirected force, inconstancy, sickness, ignorance.

ᚦ   Reactive force, directed force, vital eroticism, regenerative catalyst; or danger, defenselessness, compulsion, betrayal, dullness.

ᚠ   Divine inspiration, word-power, synthesis, transformation, intellect; or misunderstanding, delusion, manipulation by others, boredom.

ᚱ   Rationality, good advice, action, justice, ordered growth, journey; or crisis, rigidity, stasis, injustice, irrationality.

ᚲ   Artistic or technical ability, craft, transformation, offspring; or disease, decay, break-up, inability, lack of creativity.

ᚷ   Generosity, gift, magical exchange, honor, sacrifice, divine vision; or influence buying, greed, loneliness, dependence, over-sacrifice.

ᚹ   Joy, harmony, fellowship, prosperity; or stultification, sorrow, strife, alienation.

ᚺ   Change according to ideals, controlled crisis, completion, inner harmony; catastrophe, crisis, stagnation, loss of power, loss of prosperity.

ᚾ   Resistance (leading to strength), recognition of *ørlög*, innovation, need-fire (=self reliance); or constraint of freedom, distress, toil, drudgery, laxity.

ᛁ Concentrated self, ego-consciousness, self-control, unity of being; or ego-mania, dullness, blindness, dissipation.

ᛃ   Reward for positive action, plenty, peace, proper timing; or repetition, bad timing, poverty, conflict.

ᛇ   Enlightenment, endurance, initiation, protection; or confusion, destruction, dissatisfaction, weakness.

ᛈ Good omen, knowledge of *ørlög*, fellowship, and joy, evolutionary change; or addiction, stagnation, loneliness, malaise.

ᛉ   Connection with the gods, awakening, higher life, protection; or hidden danger, consumption by divine forces, loss of divine link.

ᛊ   Guidance, hope, success, goals, honor; or false goals, bad advice, false success, gullibility, loss of goals.

ᛏ   Troth (faith/loyalty), justice, rationality, self-sacrifice, analysis, victory; or mental paralysis, over analysis, over-sacrifice, injustice, imbalance.

ᛒ   Birth, becoming, life changes, shelter, liberation; or blurring of consciousness, deceit, sterility, stagnation.

ᛗ   Harmony, teamwork, trust, marriage, loyalty; or duplication, disharmony, mistrust, betrayal.

ᛙ   Divine structure, intelligence, awareness, social order, divine influence in life; or depression, mortality, blindness, self-delusion.

ᚱ   Life, passing a test, sea of vitality and of the unconscious, growth; or fear, circular motion, avoidance, withering.

◊   Resting, gestation, internal growth; or impotence, scattering, movement without change.

ᛘ   Awakening, awareness, hope/happiness, the ideal; or lack of vision, sleep, blindness, hopelessness.

ᚺ   A home, group prosperity, group order, freedom, productive interaction; or lack of customary order, totalitarianism, slavery, poverty, homelessness.

Casting Methods

Regardless of whether a casting or lay-out method is used (see above in ritual), the final matrix of meaning steads many times have common significances. The most basic form of the stead meanings is based on the special Germanic three-fold division of time and related to the function of the three great Norns. The basic significances of the three Nornic steads are:

Urðr: That which has become— the past, that which is, which exists in the objective universe, not subject to change, and at the root of the situation in question.

Verðandi: That which is becoming— the present, that which is fluctuating, which is existing in the eternal now of the subjective world, not only subject to change— but the "stuff" of change itself — and the narrow trunk of the present aspect of the situation in question.

Skuld: That which ought to (that is *should*) become given the functions of Urðr and Verðandi— the "future," that which is yet-is-not, which *may* be, the branches (or one of them) of the situation in question.

For the most profound study of the Nornic process yet ventured, see Paul C. Bauschatz, *The Well and the Tree* (Amherst: University of Massachusetts Press, 1982).

As many Runers already know, the "theory of time" posited by the Urðr-Verðandi-Skuld model or process is not the linear one of:

Past —> Present —> Future

but rather one of dynamic opposition between the vast field of significant (real) past action (Urðr) and the ever-present point of (real) existence— the synthesis of which will result in predictable channels. The vast field of "pastness" and the ever-present "nowness" are the only two realities— Skuld is a state of potentialities. This model of time accounts for many things in the traditional Germanic ideology. This includes, for example, the importance of the past and an emphasis on present action. As far as Rune-casting is concerned, a thorough intuitive understanding of these concepts will be indispensable in making meaningful readings; and the use of this pattern will be seen as the mainstay of most casting methods. This, along with the eight-fold division of the heavens, is the best indicator of the relative values of the divinatory steads of ancient Rune-casing methods.

Three-Fold Method

Follow any one of the ritual methods, and choose three staves, one at a time, and lay them out in three steads in this order:

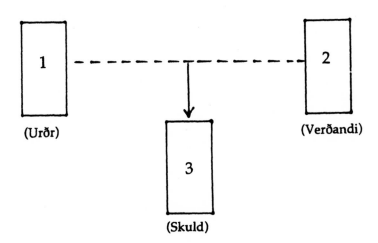

In reading this configuration first turn your attention to Urðr in its own right— what does it signify in relation to the question? Then turn your thoughts to Verðandi in a similar fashion. Now relate the Urðr and Verðandi steads and see how the Skuld stead represents a coming together of the first two.

With analytical inquiries, that is those in which the Rune-caster wishes to illuminate his or her present situation or state of being, steads 1 and 2 are of primary importance. They reveal the "present" (2) and its true background (1)— while (3) will indicate the direction things are about to go. On the other hand, in efforts to predict how things are going to be (and from the Germanic point of view of time and causality we can see this could be difficult), the Skuld-stead is primary. Skuld delivers the oracular force, while steads 1 and 2 show the foundations of this tendency. (At the same time, in "predictive" work, steads 1 and 2 show us the areas that might need magical alteration in order to avoid harmful potentialities.)

The Valknútr: A Nine-Fold Method

An expansion of the three-fold method is to be found in the *valknútr* lay-out. Again, a method of casting can be used which is then completed by picking up and laying out nine staves in the following steads and order:

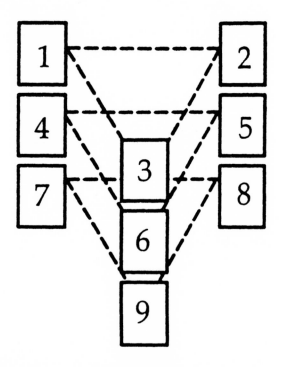

Steads 1-3 represent a detailed picture of the full process of the Urðr aspect, steads 4-6 do the same for the Verðandi aspect, while steads 7-9 show the process of Skuld as it is yet to unfold.

Because the three-fold process is so fundamental to the Germanic craft of Rune-casting, the Runer should become the master of these two techniques before venturing seriously into other methods. The Gild is highly interested in reports of trends in castings or the general records of diligent Rune-casters. There is a certain "statistical" and empirical aspect to the continued re-development of true Rune-casting.

Taking of Hail-Signs

For especially important divinatory operations we know that in elder times the Germanic peoples were not satisfied with just one method or just one message. What they wanted was corroborating evidence for the validity of the original operation. They did this by taking omens, or "hale-signs" This can be undertaken today by "learning the language of the birds." In elder times and in our Germanic homelands this could be taught with some consistent lore. But today in our dispersed condition we must make do with new methods.

The tool needed to begin to learn the language of the birds is an outdoor sacred enclosure of some size, divided into the airts of heaven. This is an area in the wide open spaces which you mark off in your imagination or in actuality. It can be of any size, but about ten yards by ten yards would be about the minimum. You should mark of the exact eight divisions of the compass. You will face north at the southern edge of your enclosure and wait for the birds "to speak." (See Figure 4.4) They will speak in two different ways: 1) with their calls, and 2) by the directions of their flight. In ancient times definite birds had definite meanings in different localities. All that can be given here are general pragmatic guidelines which can be put into practical use at once by the Runer.

Conduct such workings either between nine in the morning and three in the afternoon, or between those same hours at night. This avoids the natural activities of birds at dawn and dusk and will make significant flight or calling more obvious. Limit sitting to a definite time. This should be for no more than an hour, but no less than five minutes.

You will need to have prepared an idea of what types of birds you are likely to see or hear in your geographical area. In general, you may classify them according to their nobility or closeness to the gods and goddesses. Signs given by rarer birds are worth more (that is, they are more trustworthy) than those given by ore common birds.

The Working

Sit at the southern border of your enclosure (vé) and observe the flight of birds through the defined space and listen for the direction from which the calls of birds come. A bird flying in a certain direction is the equivalent of a call coming from that direction. The values of the airts are as follows:

Direction	World	Affirm+ Deny -	General meaning
North	Niflheimr	-	Things moving toward a restrictive state
SW	Hel	-	Static state
East	Jötunheimr	-	Chaotic state
NW	Ljóssálfheimr	+	Organized mental state
South	Muspell	-	State of dissolution
NE	Ásgarðr	+	Organized/holistic dynamic state
West	Vanaheimr	+	Organized life-force
SE	Svartálfheimr	+	Organized emotional life

In general, the use of directions to affirm or deny the validity of a reading may be over-ridden in certain circumstances. The underlying idea of this system is that the birds will give information of a specific character, which the Runer must then understand in the context of the Rune-reading. For example, let us say that a Rune-reading told you in answer to the specific question: "Should I move from my present home?" — "No, stay in your present home." For example, you could have a reading with *berkanō* or *ōþala* in the Skuld stead. Then you got a NE (Hel) indication from the birds, this could be taken as an affirming sign since they would be positively affirming the reading—*stasis*: "stay where you are."

It should be clear to Runers that this form of divination by birds could be re-developed into a complete primary form of divination. But at this stage a good deal more work must be undertaken before this could happen. Again, Runers are encouraged to explore and report on their findings.

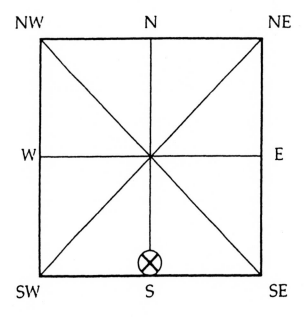

Figure 4.4: The Holy Stead for Listening to the Language of the Birds

The Fifth Door of Midgard
— Opening —

With the completion of the Fourth Door you have crossed an important threshold in your runic initiation. If you have any ambitions to enter the Rune-Gild, and you have not already done so, this might be a convenient time to write a summary report of your progress to include with an application to the Yrmin-Hall. If your Work has been thorough, the skills level which you will have attained is at the level of a Fellow of the Gild— however, in order to be so named by the Gild itself you will have to become a member and participate in the programs of the Gild for at least a year and attend at least one World-Moot.

In the Fifth Door you will expand what you have learned in the first four Doors into much more practical dimensions. You will start measuring you progress more and more against ancient Germanic lore and authentic runic tradition and against the objective world itself. It is only through the feed-back you get either from transpersonal or archetypal traditions or from the world around you that sure progress in inner development can be measured. More subjective methods easily lead to meaningless inner chatter in which nothing is learned and no real progress is made.

One of the most significantly different things between this and subsequent Doors and all previous ones is that Doors 5-9 are not keyed to a certain number of repetitions of Rune-thinking exercises which up until now have provided the pace for the work. You should spend a total of 72 days on each Door 5-9.

Reading

Suggested reading for the Fifth Door:
Now would be a good time to expand your knowledge of general magical techniques with titles such as:
Magic, W.E. Butler
The Magician, W.E. Butler
The Satanic Bible, Anton LaVey (Levey)
Also knowledge of exoteric and esoteric runology can be expanded at this time, with titles such as:
Runes and Magic, Stephen E. Flowers
Rune Games, Marijane Osborn and Stella Longland

Now would also be a good time, if you have not done so already, to become familiar with the entire neo-Germanic and even neo-Pagan movement.

Daily Work

Outwardly you will continue much as you have been. Keep to your regular schedule of work, alternating intensive periods of work with lighter periods as you feel the need.

Continue to practice every day. Even if on some days you can only do the "Daily Work of Self-Offering." Because the format of Doors 5-9 will be somewhat looser, somewhat more experimental, it is less necessary to do all of your work at one time. The Runes have been loaded in your should by now— you will be guided in the way to work that is best for you.

Yew-Work IV

There are two important additional expansions to the Yew-Work: the Mill-Work and the Road-Work.

Mill-Work

The mill-work is a method of powerfully charging the central column by activating the great horizontal wheel of the four outer spheres and their connecting beams so that it spins around like a mill-wheel— feeding the central column with increased energy.

To perform the Mill-Work the Runer should begin by activating all of the worlds within his or her personal sphere, as is usual with the Yew-Working. It is especially important to have the beams of power linking the Midgard-sphere with the outer four spheres, as shown in Figure 5.1. Once the nine spheres are powerfully present, the Runer should begin to visualize the turning of the outer spheres and the "spokes" of the wheel created by the spheres and the beams of power connecting them to Midgard. The direction of the turning should be "with the sun" (clockwise), but experiment with the widdershins direction also to note the difference in the kind of power produced. It is as if the beams are firmly attached to the outer worlds, and are detached from Midgard, but spinning around it, feeding it with increased power as the outer wheel spins. As the wheel spins faster the amount of energy being fed to the central sphere will grow, and it will begin to glow with a brighter light. Your whole being has become a dynamo— a generator of self-created fire. After the central (Midgard) sphere has been sufficiently fed, visualize the whole wheel rising up to the Ljóssálfheimr level, where the process of spinning and feeding the sphere on the axis is repeated. Ljóssálfheimr will glow and expand in power, just as Midgard had done. You will notice the increased awareness of the meanings of these worlds will grow in you as the spheres are fed.

Next, rise to the Asgard level and repeat the process.

After the Asgard sphere has been energized in this way, again work your way down to the Midgard level, and similarly work your way from there to Svartálfheimr and Hel, and from there back up to Midgard. In this process there will be a total of nine activations: Midgard three times, Ljóssálfheimr and Svartálfheimr twice each, and Asgard and Hel once each.

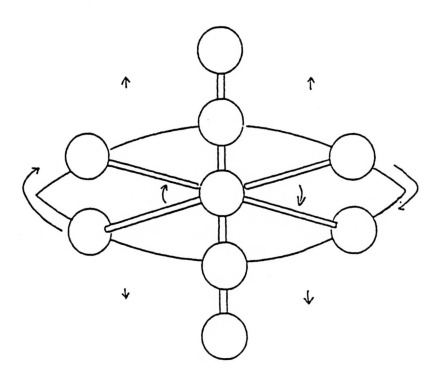

Figure 5.1: The Mill-Work

During each phase of this process, the outer wheel moves lightning quick, but the central column (axis) remains stationary. As the Runer moves the Mill-Wheel up and down the axis increased energy and power is fed to each of the spheres of the yew-column. The overall effect of this working can be *electrifying*— as the whole seems to work much like an electric generator. Energy is intensively concentrated at the point touched by the spinning "spokes" of the Mill-Wheel.

To end this exercise, return the wheel to its central position in Midgard and bring it to rest. Circulate the intensely gathered energies from the central axis throughout the psychophysical system with a series of nine or so full cycles of breath.

Road-Work

The Road-Work is the full activation of all 24 road-ways — as beams of light — among the now established nine spheres (worlds) within the greater psychophysical sphere. As your skill grows, you will be able to explore these road-ways in more detail and learn their Runes. This will be the work of future Doors.

But for right now the task is merely to establish the 24 road-ways or paths which connect the nine worlds in the subjective and objective universes. This is done by invoking the full nine spheres as with earlier phases of the Yew-Work. Now, however, you will first concentrate on the four paths leading form the outer worlds to Midgard. Make them fast in your mind's eye. Then add the paths leading from the outer four worlds to Ljóssálfheimr and Svartálfheimr. Once these are established, add the road-ways leading from the outer worlds to Asgard and Hel. Spend some time making the whole image, as shown already in Figure 4.3, firm in your mind's eye. Feel the interconnectedness of all the worlds along these 24 path-ways. The appreciation of this feeling is the realization of the Rune of "24-foldedness" which is one deeply embedded in the runic system. (This is also a mystery shared with the much neglected Hellenic system.)

Practice setting up the full array of road-ways in your personal sphere as often as you can before beginning the next Door.

With the establishment of the nine worlds and the 24 road-ways in the personal sphere, the Runer will begin to be able to feel the multidimensional web-work of wyrd in his or her very being.

Galdor III

Now that you have sung the *galdrar* of all 24 Runes over an extended period of time, and actualized their reality on a "vibratory" or sound-level it is now time to link them strongly with the visible sign of the Rune, or the Rune*stave*. This is done by visualizing the Runestave in a bright red color in your core being (in the Midgard-wheel) and in a position outside and in front of you (perhaps in the Rune-band around you). Now you sing the Rune name and/or the complete Rune galdor as learned in the last Door. When you do this visualize the Runestaves both within you and without you resonating with the power of the galdor. At that point the song and the stave become *one thing*. The stave is a picture of the sound and the sound is a reflection of the sign.

You should practice with one or more individual Runes every day during your daily work. Set up a regular schedule in your Galdor-Book which you feel comfortable with. It is probably still best to follow the fuþark order at this time in order to ensure complete and solid development of the *whole* system. Concentrate on the identity of the sign and the sound and their locations both within you and without you.

As a general note at this time, remember that you can
start to allow for bleed-over from one exercise to another at
this point in your development. Work done here will
improve your Rune-Thinking exercises, as well and
staðagaldr and Yew-Work. More and more you will be
coming to a personalized synthesis of the lore and work of
the Runes.

Staða-Work V

Through your work in the first four Doors you have now become
the master of the *forms* of the Rune-*stöður*. It is now time to amplify
this mastery. The lore of runic postures, although certainly *known* in
ancient times, was really redeveloped in the early part of this century
by the German Rune-magicians Marby and Kummer. The book *Rune-
Might* will give you further keys to using their work The Rune-Gild
program tries to put this lore into a more traditional framework and
perspective.

Surrounding the body (lyke) is a veritable leek-skin of fields of
energy. This leek- or onion-skin structure can be mined for treasures of
energy available in the zones defined by the layers. In the Yew-Work
you have been developing these layers in vocalic fields built up in the
pattern shown in figure 5.2. These are zones radiating from the vocalic
centers.

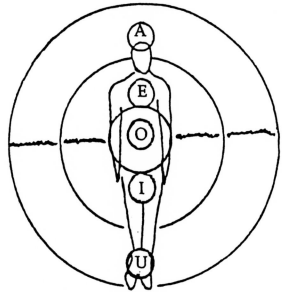

Figure 5.2: The Fields of the Leek-Skin

Using techniques already learned, and adding those learned in this Door regarding runic physiology and hand postures (see below) the Runer will be able to "tap into" these fields very efficiently.

One of the main ways to gain access to these fields of power is through the Rune-*stöður*. When you strike a runic posture note where your hands, feet, arms and legs intersect or enter into these fields of power. Feel the power enter into your core from these fields through these parts of your body. It might also be noticed that this helps to unlock some of the mysteries surrounding the actual shapes of the Runes and what these shapes mean esoterically.

An example of how the ↑-*staða* gives access to certain zones of power is shown in Figure 5.3. There we see how the arms emerge from the core and traverse the E-field and the hands enter into the A-field. Thus we can see how and why the T-stave can be a powerful channel for gaining access to the fields of Asgard and Ljóssálfheimr. From now on, when striking runic postures, the Runer should see and feel where his or her limbs are in relation to these fields of power. You can then more easily draw energy from these fields through your head, feet, arms, hands, and so on.

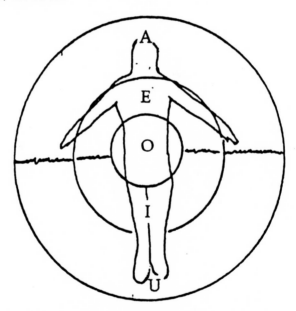

Figure 5.3: The ↑-rune Combined with the Fields of Vocalic Power

In the Fourth Door we saw how there are 24 pathways within the Yggdrasill structure surrounding and supporting the body inside and out. This is a model based on the idea of a soul structure of unseen might and main which vivifies and energizes the physical vehicle or lyke. It is well known that the ancient Germans, like their Indo-European forbears, had an esoteric doctrine in which the subtle structures of the soul were thought to have analogs in the physical body. Thus there would have been a whole doctrine of a *runic physiology*. This runic physiology is illustrated in Figure 5.4. We will leave it up to others to determine the extent to which such structures might have counterparts in physical reality— the *magical utility* of such a model is what concerns us here.

In the physical vehicle (lyke) there are veins or channels of power running from the vertical axis to the extremities. This system corresponds directly to the more subtle system of the worlds and pathways first outlined in the Fourth Door, and also outlined in *Runelore* (pp. 153-157). This internal, quasi-physical, system may prove to be a more useful alternative or augmentation to the more subtle model. With the internal system the Runer can channel energies directly from the fields of energy surrounding the body into the core. Also, these energies can be directed from the core through to the hands and feet and into the outer world to have magical effects.

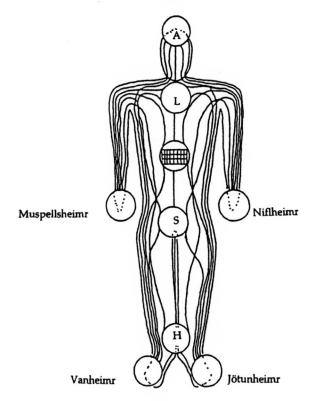

Figure 5.4: The Runic Physiology

The main immediate use for this pattern of internal runic physiology is as a conduit for runic energies making their way from the objective to the subjective realms and the reverse. This, like many other "runic models" are really magical projections from the realm of runic consciousness, and thus are quite flexible.

Höndstöður

In the use of internal runic physiology, perhaps the most important tool is that of the *hands*. These become the instruments of physical articulation in a way analogous to the way the mouth is on another level.

It was noted by some reviewers of *Futhark* that the use of magical runic hand gestures or positions was left out of the pages of that book. This kind of material is included for the *Armanen* tradition (where it is really most at home) in the pages of *Rune-Might*. I felt that it was better left out of *Futhark* because, although the use of such hand-positions seems likely to have been virtually universal among all the Indo-European peoples, there is little direct evidence remaining of it in the Germanic tradition. In *Futhark*, as generally in the *Nine Doors of Midgard*, I only include those techniques for which there is good evidence in the elder tradition. Now, that does not mean that I am against innovation— just that the basics *need* to be developed before innovation is entered into. In the first place enough people have worked with the basics of the contents of *Futhark* to warrant the expansion of knowledge to this field, and in the second place I came across some pieces of information confirming the use of magical hand gestures among the most ancient Germanic peoples.

Besides the general supposition that the form of the *elhaz*-rune may be inspired by, or reinforced by, the splayed human hand as a sign of protection or warning to potential adversaries, there is the direct evidence of a magical gesture being given by a real flesh and blood ancient Teuton. This is the Windeby girl— one of the famous so-called bog-people. Many of the bog-people were human sacrifices, and this may have been the case with the Windeby girl, but it is far more likely that she died of natural causes. She was, however, pinned down in the bog by birch branches placed over her limbs. Her eyes were blind-folded, and she was placed in such a way as to appear to be directing toward her own face a magical hand gesture similar to that sometimes called "the fig." This is done by placing the thumb between the clenched fingers of the hand. (See the Þ-rune below.) This, for the time and place of the Windeby girl, is interpreted to have been an apotropaic (protective) sign— "to ward off evil." One interpretation of all the circumstances of the Windeby girl find is that she died of natural causes, yet some one had reason to fear that she might return in the form of a walking corpse to plague the community. She was therefore treated to a special form of burial! The runic inscriptions of the elder and younger ages attest to the fact that this fear of the "walking dead," known in Old Norse as *draugar* or when awakened and sent on missions of mayhem by some magician as *dauðingar*, was well known.

Other evidence can be used to corroborate the idea that the ancient Germanic peoples had a developed system of magical hand gestures. One primary example is found on the Krogsta runestone in Sweden (from about 550 CE). It bears an image of a man holding up his hands with widely splayed fingers. Many scholars interpret this as an apotropaic sign as well. The inscription on the stone may be a personal name *Steinn*, along with a magical galdor formula. (See Flowers' *Runes and Magic*, pp. 265 *et passim* for a further discussion.)

These kinds of internal evidence, coupled with the general notion that the Germanic peoples may have shared in a tradition with their Indo-Aryan brothers inherited from some common Indo-European tradition, lead us to conclude that there is enough evidence to warrant the wider distribution of the practice of magical runic hand-positions, or *höndstöður*. (Among the Indians these gestures are usually called *mudras*.)

Now that you have progressed this far in the practice of *stöður*, know the trials and tribulations of the practice of *stöður*. Magically speaking, the *höndstöður* can accomplish very similar if not identical results as the full body *stöður*. The *höndstöður* have the great advantage, however, of being able to be performed in virtually any location, at any time, without drawing undue attention to yourself. Furthermore, these practices will develop and concentrate magical power in the *hands* of the Runer. This can also be of great traditional advantage, as the hands are considered to be storehouses of energy and points of projection of such energies into the environment or its withdrawal from other beings. In the practice of runic *höndstöður*, the Runer is to visualize the power of the Rune, contained in a sphere around the hand or hands engaged in performing the *staða*. As the section above on runic physiology has shown, these spheres are the equivalents of the cosmic worlds of Muspellsheimr (in the right hand) and Niflheimr (in the left hand), and there are streams or rivers of controlling force connecting the power centers of the hands with the other power centers along the central Yew-column. The connection with the Midgard center is especially useful, of course.

It can not be over emphasized that you should experiment with *höndstaða* variations. It is really only of vital importance that you develop a set of 24 hand postures that *feel right* to you, to practice with them, and make them *your own*. With those signs that require only one hand, try using the left and the right hands and see which one feels better to you. Note the differences, if any, in your Galdor-Book. As far as the tradition is concerned, some of the following *stöður* were taken from ancient Germanic clues, some from the *Armanen* tradition, and some are the result of personal experiments by the Yrmin-Drighten. For more information on the history of Runic hand postures, see S. A. Kummer's *Rune-Magic* published by Rûna-Raven.

It is suggested that you substitute *höndstöður* exercises for full *staða* work in the curriculum, or add them in a way that parallels the scheduling of the full *staða* work. You are also encouraged to practice *höndstöður* in various odd moments to build your sense of runic power and concentration of that power.

These *höndstöður* are especially valuable in the practice of *Rune-fixing*. Now that you have a deep level sense for the meanings of the Runes, and have some sense of their inner coherent "meta-language," you will have experiences in which perhaps while walking along, you will suddenly be struck by an image in your environment, or even a subjective feeling will roll up from within, and you will think: "That's what the so-and-so Rune feels like!" At that moment you would like to have a way to fix that feeling or perception, or image with the Rune in question so that perhaps you could re-evoke it at will at a later time under controlled magical circumstances. The *höndstöður* are an ideal way of doing this. When such a perception comes, the Runer has but to make the hand-sign *while you have the perception*— and it will thereby be fixed in the psychosomatic complex of the Runer. These build up, are stored up, and can be utilized at a later time under the will of the Runer.

Descriptions of the *Höndstöður*

Here follow the descriptions of the 24 *höndstöður*. They are also all illustrated in the following Figures 5.1-24. Variations on some of these can be found in *Rune-Might*.

1. To make the F-rune the left arm is lifted vertically with the index, middle and small fingers vertical as well, with the thumb and ring finger slanted out parallel to the right. Sign of the horns may be substituted with the right hand.

2. The *ûruz* is made with the thumb and index finger forming the U-rune with the other fingers forming a flat surface with the index finger. The direction of the opening of the Rune should be toward the ground. Sign of the horns with the left hand may be substituted.

3. The *þurisaz* is made by placing the thumb between either the index and middle, or middle and ring fingers (as shown), of the clenched fist. The thumb should stick out a bit from between the fingers, thus forming the "thorn."

4. To make the A-rune, you can close the tips of the thumb and index finger to form a circle. The other fingers can be held out straight (as shown in the figure), or be curved around with the other fingers.

5. The *raiðō* Rune is made by clenching the thumb inside a fist of closed fingers. You can experiment with the left or right hand. A variant sign is shown in *Rune-Might*, where the left index finger and thumb close to make a ring with the other fingers of the left hand slanting down at the base of the thumb.

6. The K-rune is made by creating a right-angle between the fingers of your left hand in a flat plane and the left thumb.

7. The *gebō* Rune is made by interlocking the fingers of both hands right at their bases, such that an X-shape is formed. The thumbs should also be crossed. The sign can be held overhead, at chest level, or in the genital region. Experiment holding the right thumb over the left, and the left thumb over the right, also.

8. The W-rune is formed by closing the tip of the thumb together with the tips of the ring and little fingers, with the other fingers straight. Point the index and middle fingers downward. Experiment with both the right and left hands. The right hand may be considered the standard here.

9. *Hagalaz* is formed by holding the tips of both thumbs together with all the fingers of both hands held at right angles to the thumbs straight up. Your hands may be held in front of you at chest level, or high overhead.

10. The N-rune is formed by the two index fingers crossing one another at the second knuckle. The left finger is held straight up, while the left index finger crosses it (either in front or behind) at a 45 degree angle. The other fingers are clenched in a fist.

11. The *isa* Rune is simply formed by holding the index finger upright with the other fingers in a fist. Try it with the right and left hands.

12. To form the *jēra* Rune, the thumb and fingers of both hands are closed to about 45 degrees, and the fingers of one hand are placed between the thumb and fingers of the other hand to form the interlocking image of the J-rune. Do not let one hand touch the other during the performance of this sign.

13. The *ihwaz* Rune is made by interlocking the index, middle and ring fingers of both hands and having the tips the little fingers and thumbs touch. It is best to press very hard with the thumbs and little fingers to the full impact of the two points of consciousness, above and below. The hands should be held in front of the solar plexus region.

14. The P-rune is formed by holding the palms of both hands together, thumbs parallel to each other. The middle and ring fingers are folded down leaving the little and index fingers upright.

15. To form the Y-Rune, stretch the thumb, index and middle fingers of the left or right hand (or both!). The index finger is at a right angle to the earth. The other fingers are clenched. A variation is simply the splayed hand with all five fingers spread out as widely as possible.

16. The S-rune is made by holding the left hand with the fingers and thumb in a right angle, and having the tip of the middle finger of the right hand touching the tip of the left thumb, thus forming the *sowilō* shape. Hold it at eye level or above your head.

17. To form the T-rune, the tips of the middle fingers on both hands are held in a house-top shape. This is the vault of the sky. The tips of the thumbs are held together to form the plane of the earth.

18. The *berkanō* Rune is formed by holding the thumb of the right hand in the clenched fist of the left hand, with the left fist on top of the right one. This emphasizes the aspect of concealment. Or, you can just place the left fist over the right (as shown).

19. The E-rune is made by placing the tips of both index fingers against one another at the tip of the finger nail, while each is bent as two horse heads facing one another. The other fingers are clenched in a fist.

20. *Mannaz* is formed by crossing the index fingers of both hands at the second knuckle while touching the tips of one index finger to the tip of the other thumb. The other fingers must find a comfortable position, they may be interlocked with one another if necessary.

21. The *laguz* is made by simply bending the fingers down at the second knuckle to from a crook. The thumb is held flat with the palm. Use the right hand or the left.

22. *Ingwaz* is formed by making a diamond shape by touching the tips of both thumbs and the tips of both middle fingers together. The sign may be held overhead, at the solar plexus region, or in the genital area.

23. *Dagaz* is formed by interlocking two A-rune signs (thumb and index finger closed in a circle). The position of the other fingers is unimportant. Just keep from actually making physical contact between one hand and the other when making the sign.

24. The O-rune is made by the thumbs and index fingers of both hands. Index fingers pointing downward and the other fingers clenched in a fist. The tips of the thumbs are touching and the fingers are crossed at the second knuckle. Make the sign in front of you, or overhead.

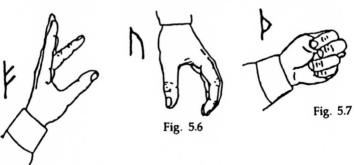

Fig. 5.6

Fig. 5.7

101

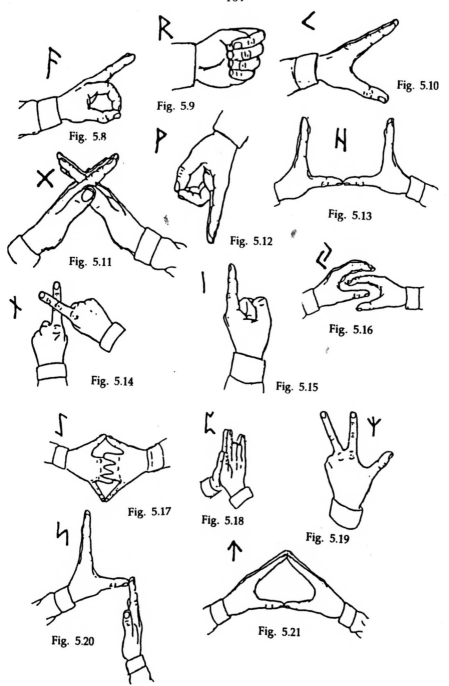

Fig. 5.8

Fig. 5.9

Fig. 5.10

Fig. 5.11

Fig. 5.12

Fig. 5.13

Fig. 5.14

Fig. 5.15

Fig. 5.16

Fig. 5.17

Fig. 5.18

Fig. 5.19

Fig. 5.20

Fig. 5.21

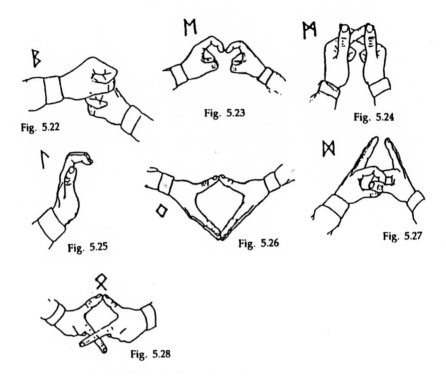

Fig. 5.22

Fig. 5.23

Fig. 5.24

Fig. 5.25

Fig. 5.26

Fig. 5.27

Fig. 5.28

Rune-Thinking V

Now you have not only established the traditional forms of the Runes in your mind, but you have also deeply imbibed the oldest and most traditional seeds of expanded runic wisdom still available to us in the form of the Rune poems. You are now fully prepared to let you mind wander freely in the Rune realms, and you may be fully confident that what you find there will be of great validity and power.

At this point you should take time in each of your daily workings to contemplate an individual Rune. Spend as much time as you like on this— as long as it is beneficial. At this stage you may find that the runic channels are so widely opened that thoughts and insights come like flashes of lightning and that days of work can be done in split second realizations.

Turn your attention to one Rune each day. As this Door should take about 72 days to complete, you have time to spend a total of an average of three days per Rune. However, there is no need to create a strict schedule here. You may need or want to spend more time on one Rune than another at this stage.

To do this free-form runic contemplation just use the techniques that you have found most useful up to now, whether it is singing the galdor or just visualizing the Runestave, to get your mind on the track of the Rune in question. But once this *engagement* has been established and felt, let your mind be free of all bonds and fetters. The only restriction is one that you yourself will impose: if you feel yourself loosing the feel of engagement with the runic stream as you have come to know it, retrack yourself using the same technique you used to get yourself engaged to begin with.

It is most important at this stage that you record all of your results faithfully in your Galdor-Book.

Over the years in my own Galdor-Books I have recorded many findings. Years later I will go back to them and I find that things I discovered in such contemplations fall into several categories in retrospect. Some will have become so much a part of my thinking that I am sometimes surprised and not seldom delighted to re-discover the point of their origin, others are seen to be confirmed by subsequent academic research, while some others appear now to be utter nonsense— although they *seemed* profound at the time. The most interesting and useful of such records are, however, those which make more sense *now* than they did *then*. Seeds are buried in your Galdor-Book. These seeds gestate and if you go to find them later they will provide good food for thought.

The actual forms that realizations about the Runes might take are really dependent on how your own mind and faculties of inspiration have developed. Some make findings in the form of geometrical diagrams, others in (praeter)-natural scenes, others in words and verbal formulas. As the true Runes are unlimited by natural forms, they can take many forms under such circumstances. It is your inner sense of their ultimate forms that will guide you in these contemplations.

Taufr II

(Talismanic Magic)

You have now gained basic experience in the carving of Runes and in the talismanic execution of each of the 24 Runes of the Elder Fuþark. These were the foundations of all that will follow.

The essence of how basic *taufr* magic works is contained in the threefold formula:

1) stave
2) song
3) Rune

The working of true *taufr* consists of the correct knowledge and crafting of these three elements. The **stave** is the **shape** of the actual runic sign (or bind-rune, *galdrastafr*, etc.). The **song** is the form of the sound formula (usually vocal or verbal) that is used to load the shape.

The **Rune** is the actual **hidden lore** which is the Rune itself (not just the external form of the stave or sound). This threefold essence: shape, sound, lore (information) acts as a complex lens or focusing mechanism for the will. When a form of threefold concentration and focusing of will is achieved the magical effects being directed by the will through these tools will be far more likely to succeed.

Continue to practice with the writing or carving of individual Runes, runic formulas, and even bind-runes. Carve or write them with full attention and awareness while singing the names or other galdor formulas (either out loud or silently in your head). At the same time these things are going on, let as much as you know of the runic mystery itself drift through your head and flow into the shape and sound of the Rune-stave and Rune-song.

Ideally, you would draw or carve one stave (Runestave, bind-rune, or galdor-stave) every day loading it with all Your might and main. Record the results of your work in the Galdor-Book. You might want to keep the staves that are especially well executed, while those that are not quite to your liking can be destroyed by fire in the fire-pot. In the process or loading them you make the staves into magical objects, and so they must be treated with respect and care.

Obviously the work you are doing in galdor and Rune-thinking will feed this practice, as it feeds them. In this, as in most avenues of Rune-work, we are approaching the craft from a wide variety of diverse angles and grasping the power and knowledge of the Runes within the vast net-work of our hearts and minds.

Runecasting III
(Runic Divination)

We know that the Rune poems presented in Door III originally come from a tradition of runic divination. In fact the whole practice of Germanic alliterative verse (discussed in Door III) probably has its roots in the practice of runic divination. The poetic stanzas corresponding to the Rune-names acted as mnemonic devices to help the Runecaster remember the lore of the Rune. Also the stanzas acted as oracular sayings which could be read in the context of a question being put to the Rune-staves thus illuminating the question. You have used the Rune poems to illuminate you up till now— now it is time to turn that inner illumination to the purpose of helping you to clarify questions in the subjective and objective universe.

In practical terms you will now simply recite the stanza of a Rune poem corresponding to each of the Runes you come up with in an operation of Runecasting. Recite it, reflect on it, and **read** it in the light of the question. Try to experiment using **only** the poetic stanzas of the Rune poems in making Rune readings for a while. Record your results in the Galdor-Book. After a period of experimentation you may go to a system in which you use a mixture of key-words or other mnemonic devices and the traditional runic stanzas. It is in this aspect that the practice of Runecasting most closely approaches the oracular quality of the *I-Ching*, for example.

Although the Rune poems as they have come down to us historically are invaluable mainstays of **traditional** runic lore, we must at the same time recognize that they are far from the original Rune poems used in the oldest times. The Old English Rune Poem undoubtedly contains changes made due to Christian influence, the Old Norwegian and Old Icelandic poems, of course, represent the Younger Tradition, and so do not address the same set of symbols as were represented in the Elder Fuþark. The Old Norwegian and Old Icelandic poems are, however, more purely Heathen in their tone and content. A comparison of all the poems will show that they all stem from a now lost common original tradition.

As an exercise in your capacity runically to synthesize the lore you have learned, and to do so in a traditional manner so that it may be useful to others, I now recommend that you write your own version of a Rune poem based on the 24 Runes of the Elder Fuþark. In doing this exercise, you should take the contents of all of the known Rune poems into account, and couple this with what else you know of Runelore— both from other branches of the tradition and what you have been able to glean from personal experience. The poetic tradition is not a theater for the absolutely free expression of the individual and for individual "creativity."

To give an example of this, I present a New Rune Poem in modern English, which I wrote at this stage of my own development.

A New Rune Poem

ᚠ (Fee) will flow   to all who freely give;
    before the Lord and Lady 'tis good lot,
       for it is the fire of life—
but the snake's red sheath   is the strife of men.

ᚢ (Urus) is an awful might   and a fierce main—
high are his horns   and hard to stop—
but drizzle is dreaded   by the hardness of ice.

ᚦ (Thurs) is a dreaded fiend   who brings fearsome doom:
    yet doughty Thunar can best him,
       for the hammer is harder than rock—
but it is not good to grasp   this gruesome thorn.

ᚠ (Ase) is the All-Father   who dwells in Asgard:
          he guides the wise along the ways,
          and wields the might the word—
but to those unredy   he gives a wretched road all-wroth.

ᚱ (Riding) is right for warriors   along the road to wisdom;
          for those in the hall 'tis good rede,
          it rolls as a rowel on a wain—
but for the horse   it is rough and hard.

ᚲ (Keen) is kent by its fire   and 'tis mild to all kin:
          it heats the forge and hearth,
          it gives light to the lords—
but 'tis a canker if wild   and wounds the flesh.

ᚷ (Gift) is help to the guest   who gambols into the hall;
          by his gar we know the god
          who gave the first gift of ghost—
but a gift looks   on the gallows for gain.

ᚹ (Wyn) is happiness and wonder   for those without woes;
          it is blessedness and a boon
          to all kinsmen in the clan—
but without wisdom   wyn becomes woeful.

ᚺ (Hail) is the coldest grain   and the whitest stone of heaven;
          it was hard on wheat,
          and yet worse for worms—
but from the stone   did Sig-Father shape the world.

ᚾ (Need) is narrow   on the naked heart—
          it is tiresome toil,
          it bores and then it burns—
but from its working   are wonders wrought.

ᛁ (Ice) make the iron   that comes in the world,
          and a floor that's o'er the flux
          it gleams like a gem all-dear—
but it dooms with death   those who deal with it lightly.

ᛃ (Year) is good and gained   when the grain is harvested;
          to all bairns 'tis a boon
          when the lord's seed is sown
          and good speed is gained—
but if deeds are dire   the doom is dreaded.

ᛇ (Yew) stands hard   in the midst of the yard;
     far within there flames a fire,
        it lives many years and long—
but eats a bairn its berries   it will be his bale.

ᛈ (Perth) is a peg   for earnest play
     it shows all the shape
       of ordeals of athelings—
but it can weaken   a good soul's wit.

ᛉ (Elks) are awful   in the ash of the world;
     worrisome to untried warriors,
    but winsome to the wise—
and red is the road   that is ridden by the Runer.

ᛋ (Sun) leads us o'er the seas   with all good speed,
     her light doth lead us upward;
      'neath the stone slithers the snake—
but if the soul is sorry   naught comes of the sea.

ᛏ (Tiw) holds troth well   with athelings good and true;
    he rightly tallies the tides,
      and sits amidst the northern sky—
but he betokens woe   for those who break the troth-bonds.

ᛒ (Birch) is brightest   at the blessing of spring;
     birth she gives to bairns
    buried deep in her burrow—
but blurry becomes life   for those who withhold the bowl.

ᛖ (Eean) is an earnest friend   to earls and athelings
    bent on great deeds and doings
    together the two are true—
but sundered from the soul   the earl sinks in sorrow.

ᛗ (Man) is the gladness   of mankind's deep memories;
     in Middelert is mildness known
     as the mead fills the mind—
but moods become murky   when mildness is lost.

ᛚ (Lake) is the water of life   and the law of ordeal
    ruled by the lord and lady,
      in love grows the leek—
but the waves unheeded   will drown the wanderer.

◊ (Ing) is the lord of earth   who eastward fared
        with his wain o'er the wave:
        riches are his reward—
but fruitless are farings   without the lord's frith.

ᛘ (Day) is dear   to drightens and dolts;
        light is dealt by lot;
      darkness is lifted by deeds—
but death is the doom   for him who dreads day.

ᛦ (Odle) is ringed with oak   and warded all-round,
       in frith and freedom lives the folk,
       riches follow what is right—
but if the ring is wretched   woe will be the winnings.

This can be used for oracular purposes, or such poems can just act as synthetic keys to your own knowledge of the Runes. The writing of your own Rune poem will itself be a powerful tool for your own transformation into a Rune-Master.

The material in *Runecaster's Handbook* provides the Runer with ideas for expansion of the techniques of Runecasting. But with all of the complexities of form, if the basics have not been learned *from within* the results of your Runecastings will be less than *full of truth*.

The Sixth Door of Midgard
— Opening —

With the completion of the Fifth Door you are well on your way to the practical implementation of Rune-wisdom and Rune-work in your daily life. The Runes will have become a part of your very thought process.

Since the runic patterns, the very principles upon which each of the Runes is based, have become a part of your thinking, the following exercise might be interesting to carry out at this time. Turn your "runic eye" — your deepest level of understanding of the principles of the mysteries the Runestaves represent — to the world and society around you. See what best symbolizes the runic principle for you in contemporary society. An example of this would be the way in which the automobile has assumed the ancient role of the horse (*ehwaz*) not only in our material culture, but also in the hidden symbolic culture as well. As an experiment, create your own system of contemporary "Rune names" to correspond to the ancient system.

Reading

For this Door the Runer should read the works in category 6 of the bibliography which have not yet been read. Special attention should be given to the esoteric aspects and possibilities of the "trifunctional" ideas presented by Georges Dumézil. These ideas can be applied to the living present reality of the individual and to the society in which we now live— except they now constitute a hidden and even unconscious tradition, rather than a consciously established set of principles. It is this loss of awareness about how our culture is supposed to function in a healthy way that is often found to be at the root of present-day social and cultural problems.

Daily Work

In this Door you will be introduced to the hidden or secret practice of blessing (invocation of an entity and a sacrificial offering to that entity). This is a tool in the storehouse of magical techniques the true Runer must eventually master. Some will find this technique highly useful while others will find it less so— much as *staðagaldr* is sometimes found to be. For the period of the next two Doors I recommend that you carry out a ritual invocation of some kind on a daily or near daily basis.

For anyone interested in the regular practice of Germanic religion, and its rituals, *A Book of Troth* (2003) is highly recommended. The methods of inner working learned in the Nine Doors program can be applied directly to making the rites contained in *A Book of Troth* more effective.

Yew-Work V

In the last Door you learned how to energize the various realms within the psychophysical complex along the vertical axis of the yew-column and how to construct the web-work of roadways throughout your system. By now the Runer should have a very good idea of, and feeling for, the essences of all nine worlds of the Yggdrasill framework. It is now time to put that knowledge and intuition to work in further analyzing the Runes as they actually live in your being.

This will be developed even further in Doors 8-9 in the form of actual Road-Wending, but for right now more narrowly runic work will be the order of the day.

Once you have firmly established and realized the presence of the nine worlds in your personal system by undertaking the road-working as outlined in the last Door, begin to concentrate on just one road-way per day. Start with those connecting the five worlds of the Yew-column, then go on to those leading from Midgard to the outer four worlds, then those leading from the outer worlds to Ljóssálfheimr and Svartálfheimr, and finally on those leading from the outer realms to Asgard and Hel. Pick one each day and contemplate the connection between the two worlds in question. Feel what the first realm means, then feel what the other realm means to you— and finally feel what the connection, the synthesis of these two worlds feels like. Do not try to restrain yourself with thought and analysis— let everything you now about the worlds come together in a free flowing way. Fix this feeling in your heart.

The next step is to see which Rune matches most closely the feeling you have fixed in your heart which describes the connection between any two worlds. In this way you will be able to build of a set of correspondences between the 24 Runes of the Elder Fuþark and the 24 road-ways running among the nine worlds of Yggdrasill.

Note the correspondences in your Galdor-Book. Concentrate on just one road-way per day. In the 72 days of this Door you will have time to come back to each of the road-ways three times. After this cycle is completed you should have a solid set of correspondences. The Gild is very much interested in the results of these exercises. If you have ever seen any "traditional" correspondences between the Runes and the paths of the Yggdrasill pattern, these should be ignored for the sake of your own personal work.

One way to fix the feelings you have for each of the road-ways is to assign a color correspondence to it (and thus to the Rune which seems to belong to that pathway). When you fully realize the prismatic splendor of such an array of correspondences, you will perceive for the first time directly what the mystery of the Bifröst Bridge truly is. It is the bridge, the universal linkage between and among all the worlds— symbolized as the Rainbow (or the electromagnetic spectrum for those who wish to "up-date" the eternally true metalanguage).

Another thing you might want to spend some time contemplating at this point is the way in which the outer sphere, or orb, creates a subtle connection among all of the outermost realms: Asgard-Hel-Jötunheimr-Vanaheimr-Niflheimr-Muspellsheimr. The interconnections between and among these worlds can only be indirectly intuited, as there are no direct runic keys which link them together. The reality of this orb is symbolically contained in the outer Rune-ring or Rune-band which encircles the orb at its "equator." This is the mystery of the Midgard-Serpent which encircles and contains the cosmos— this is also why Runes are so often found carved inside the band-work created by the body of serpents on Runestones. The outer-serpent is a reflection on the face of the orb of the inner-serpent who dwells in the heart of every Runer.

The prismatic array of colors contained in the many road-ways is also reflected in the orb, where is creates another form of the Bifröst Bridge— linking the inner worlds to the outer orb.

In the next Door we will learn how to activate this system in an operative way.

Rune-Thinking VI

Now that you have spend some time contemplating individual Runes, it is time to move on to similar contemplations of runic combinations.

The methods developed in the Fifth Door contemplations of individual Runes may be applied here as well. But because long ground work has not necessarily been laid for the outer forms of the combinations outlined here, it will probably be necessary to spend a few moments establishing an outer form for the runic combinations, and from these forms you will be able to engage the bound runic streams in a way identical to the way you engage single runic streams.

In this Door, you will contemplate various natural runic combinations of two and three Runestaves. By natural combinations I mean that their bond is suggested in the very structure of the Fuþark itself.

Such combinations would be those made by taking every two Runes in paired sequence through the Fuþark, F+U, Þ+A, R+K, etc., the pairs made by the division of the Fuþark into two rows of 12 laid side to side (see *Runelore* p. 148), the pairs made by the Runes complementing each other when in the complete Fuþark Rune-ring, as shown in Figure 6.1.

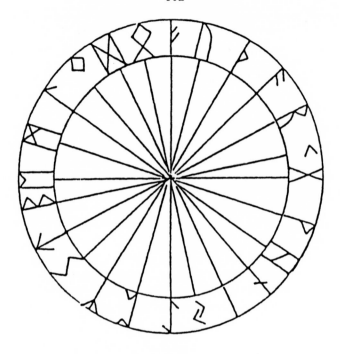

Figure 6.1: Ring of Runic Complements

Threefold combinations are also naturally suggested by the three vertical Runes in the *ætt*-pattern, F+H+T, U+N+B, etc., or by taking each group of three Runes in Fuþark sequence, F+U+Þ, A+R+K, etc.

These are just a few of the most obvious, and therefore basically meaningful, combinations you might want to investigate from an inner perspective.

Before beginning this phase you should make up a schedule of some sort so that you can be as systematic as possible about this. Take one kind of combination and see it through from beginning to end. The work done in this field will also be very valuable in the development of skills in Rune-reading for divinatory purposes.

The technique for this kind of contemplation would involve the Runer first visualizing the two or three Runes in question, and then arranging them (in your imagination or on paper) in some combined form. This may take the shape of a bind-Rune, or some other arrangement of the Runes. Then engage the combined runic stream in the way you would a single Rune, sing a combined galdor, and visualize the bind-Rune or other combined form. Just let the images or thoughts well up from within, as you would with a single Rune. Again record all your realizations in the Galdor-Book.

Staða-Work VI

The foundations of *staðagaldr* are now fully laid. It is now time to begin to experiment with more operative methods of using this form of Rune-galdor.

In theory *staðagaldr* works in pretty much the same way as other forms of "Rune-magic." Its advantage is that it works directly with and within, and from out of the body as its actual magical medium. It turns motion and gesture into media for magical expression.

The first forays into operative *staðagaldr* best take the forms of traditional runic formulas. Again in theory any working that can be done by means of *taufr* can be undertaken with *staðagaldr*.

Workings of *Staðagaldr*

To begin any formal working of *staðagaldr*, you should at minimum perform the Yew-Working to quicken and kindle the energies of your soul. However, you might want to perform all of the preparatory work you would do in the working of a formal act of *taufr*-magic. The only difference is that instead of carving the Runes into wood with your knife or rister, you carve them directly into the fabric of the objective universe with your gestures and motions. The performance of the galdors or incantations are virtually the same in both forms.

The traditional formulas of *alu*, *laukaz*, *ehwaz*, *luwatuwa*, etc. provide the framework for the first experiments in operative *staðagaldr*. The Runer should, after making any ritual preparations he or she finds necessary to the working, perform the standing of each Rune in sequence of the chosen formula. If the *alu* formula has been chosen, the A-Rune standing should be performed (complete with the galdor of that Rune), then the Runer smoothly moves into the L-Rune posture and sings the galdor of the Rune, and finally the Runer moves into the U-Rune posture and sings the galdor of that stave. This process can be repeated as often as the Runer feels is necessary until the full effect of the formula can be felt to have "clicked in." One of the main reasons why we strongly suggest that the Runer use the traditional runic formulas in various initial experiments in operative runic techniques is that you will gain a deep sense for how the Rune should feel— and thus you will be able to tell for yourself when you have truly engaged the runic streams. Besides, the traditional formulas will give you a deeper insight and experience in the oldest and most basic forms of Rune-magic than any free-form approach might give.

Experiment with all of the traditional runic formulas you know. Do a different one every day and keep a record in the Galdor-Book as to how each one makes you feel, how it compares to the way other experiments with the same formula makes an impact, etc.

Taufr III
(Talismanic Magic)

The very acts of risting, rowning, and reddening (carving, chanting and coloring) the Runes make up the simplest and most effective elements of the practice of *taufr* magic. However, some Runers may feel the need for a more elaborate form of runic ritual to give themselves more symbolism and activity in which to express their magical wills more fully. This need is recognized by the extensive ritual for charging a runic talisman given in *Futhark* (pp. 112-116).

The basic steps in such a ritual are:

1. Opening: Perform a Hammer-, Hail-, or *Elhaz*-Working.
2. Galdor: Sing the form of the Rune-song (galdor)
   relevant to the working before beginning the drawing
   or carving. In the case of a single Rune this would be
   the Rune-name and the galdor of the Rune.
3. Risting (carving): Carve or draw the shape of the Rune-
   stave, Rune-row, or bind-Rune while rowning (singing)
   the name of the Rune being carved.
4. Reddening (coloring): Paint or inlay the carved shapes
   with pigment or other coloring (red is always the
   preferred color). If you are drawing the staves with a
   pen you should use red ink. In such cases the risting
   and reddening are simultaneous operations.
5. Hiding (enclosure): Cover the talismanic object with a
   black cloth and bind it nine times around with a string
   or thong. This directs the runic powers to an inner
   from which they will be able to emerge in full
   activity. Feel the runic powers descending into a realm
   of darkness where they will gather strength from depths
   of power yet unknown. You may compose a word-formula
   which expresses this idea and recite it over the
   enclosed talismanic object.
6. Birth (emergence): Unbind and uncover the object and
   feel the great outrush of power as it is given birth
   in the world of objective reality. Again speak words
   that illustrate the fact of the birth of the *taufr* in
   the world were it will do its work.
7. Naming: This is an optional step. If you want the *taufr*
   to have a long term effect, you may want to reinforce
   the fact that this is a living magical entity, and one
   with its own *ørlög*, by giving it a name as you would a
   new-born child. Pass the *taufr* over a flame three
   times, and sprinkle it with water as you pronounce the
   chosen name over it.

8. Loading (charge): Now you state in clear and certain
   what the fate and mission of the *taufr* is to be. At
   this time also visualize the end results of the magical
   operation— see them as already completed. In the
   grammar of the loading you might also want to put all
   the verbs in the past tense to reemphasize this point.
9. Fastening (sealing): In order to hold the loading to the
   talisman, you will want to trace a ring around the
   form three times while visualizing a sphere around it
   holding the might and main to the object.
10. Closing: Perform a ritual closing in accordance with the
   way you opened the rite.

Inner *Taufr*-Work

When you are actually carving or drawing a Rune-stave you may
begin to incorporate what you are learning about the inner Yggdrasill
by guiding runic powers from your central core out through your arm
and hand actually doing the carving or drawing. Fundamental to this is
an understanding of the "runic physiology" presented in the Fifth Door.

Begin by using the same technique you have learned to use in
signing and sending the Runes. Formulate the runic power in your
center and project it out through your arm and hand— through the
rister (or other tool) and into the object you are carving or drawing on.
Later, once the runic physiology and the internal Yggdrasill have been
more fully established in your being, you may begin to lead the runic
powers from the various locations within the tree out through your
hand and into the object being carved.

Galdor IV

Galdor-work has now almost become second nature for you. The
Runes have begun to sing and hum in the very core of your being— the
mysteries are coming alive within you. Before going on to operative
magical work that is highly personalized to you, it is the best course to
realize and activate the ancient Rune-songs that have come down to us
in the body of runic inscriptions.

When you sing these galdors, sing them with absolute attention to
each of the individual Runes that make up the formula. Treat each one
as if it were the only Rune in your mind at the time. At that moment
only that Rune exists. Then the whole is re-synthesized as the entire
formula is put back together.

As an example of how this work is done, I will outline the procedure
with the *ALU*-formula. As you already know, *alu* is an ancient word
for magical and inspirational power (which became attached to the
ritual substance sometimes used to raise this power— ale). As Runers
we can "drink the ale of inspiration" by runic means alone.

First sing the whole formula a few times (three, or nine times are most traditional): *alu-alu-alu*, then sing each individual Rune in the formula: *ansuz-laguz-uruz*, and then sing the formula one more time in a prolonged fashion: *aaaalllllluuuuuu*. When you sing the introductory series, let your mind settle on the meaning of the whole formula. Recall all of your associations with it. When you sing the individual Rune names concentrate totally on the meanings of those names only. Finally, when you put it all together for the final singing of the galdor, let the meanings of the whole formula and the meanings of the individual Runes flow together in a magical whole. As you are intoning the "a" sound, visualize the A-Rune, as you are intoning the "l" sound, visualize the L-Rune, and as you are intoning the "u" sound, visualize the U-Rune.

Practice several times with the *alu*-formula before going on to other traditional galdor-formulas. During the course of this Door, you should repeat the work with the *laukaz*, *auja*, *gibu auja*, and *luwatuwa* formulas. Spend a few days on each one.

All of these formulas are performed on the tape *Rune-Song*.

Blessing-Work I
Runic Uses of Invocation

Calls to the Lesser Wights

The runic technology of the blessing (ON *blót*, pl. *blótar*) or ritual sacrifice can be important to certain kinds of Rune-galdor. For example, when loading a Rune-tine the Runer may actually transform the tine into a living creature with a specific wyrd (destiny) to fulfill. In such operations, the tine itself will have a name and in this name it will be born and called upon in a ritual modeled on the one given here for dwarves, elves or etins. Many Runers may also find it intrinsically useful to gain familiarity with the form of galdor contained in the ritual form of the blessing. For more information on the various forms of the blessing rite and its use in the common troth of the Germanic peoples, see *A Book of Troth*.

There is a runic (hidden) process which can go on in any work of blessing. In order for the galdor to work as well as it possibly can, the Runer must approach this rite and its actions with the utmost powers of concentration and visualization. The words you speak are galdors, the actions you perform are *staðagaldr* in motion. The process is an internal runic one symbolized in external actions and words.

To perform a ritual blessing the Runer will need a harrow (altar), a blessing bowl (preferably wooden) and if the rite is performed indoors an auxiliary bowl, a horn or other drinking vessel, a sprig of evergreen, and some form of liquid drink. For the drink mead or ale are most traditional, but other forms may be substituted. These items are to be arranged as shown in Figure 6.2.

Figure 6.2: The Harrow Arrangement for a Ritual Blessing

The inner process is essential to the working of the blessing as a form of galdor. This inner process is illustrated in Figure 6.3. There we see that the mead is loaded from three sources: 1) the verbal formulas spoken into it, 2) the actions performed with and around it, and 3) the essential (symbolic or substantial) power contained in it. This latter source is especially strong when traditional forms of liquid — especially those which have been brewed for expressly magical purposes — are used. This power is channeled through the horn (or other drinking vessel) wherein it is loaded with further mytho-magical powers through the formulas spoken and actions performed. From the horn the power is split into one stream flowing into and throughout the being of the Runer (and other participants), and into another stream flowing into the blessing bowl standing on the harrow. The power directed into the inner being of the Runer empowers the subjective universe, while that directed into the bowl on the harrow is being prepared for continuing work in the objective universe outside the Runer. From the bowl the power is divided into two parts: 1) to hallow the Runer and the world, and 2) to act as a gift (sacrifice) to the entity being invoked in the rite. The first part of the power is taken out through the organic (arboreal) symbol of the evergreen twig and through this agency the power is distributed to the outside of the Runer and to the surface of the harrow. This act hallows (protects and empowers) the Runer and the world, which is symbolized by the harrow. The second part of the power contained in the bulk of the mead remaining in the bowl is "grounded" back into the earth— giving the power to the wight being invoked.

It should be noted that the Runer gains access to this power from two directions, from the inside and from the outside. These two meet in the midst of the Runer's magical being and empower him from both extremes of the realms within and without.

In the course of the blessing the power of divine consciousness and being (manifest in the mead) is circulated through the human body and soul, and throughout symbols of the other "kingdoms" or realms of existence — animal, vegetable and mineral. Thus a whole "ecology of power" is represented in the formula of the blessing. This is a general formula that can be adapted for many purposes of galdor.

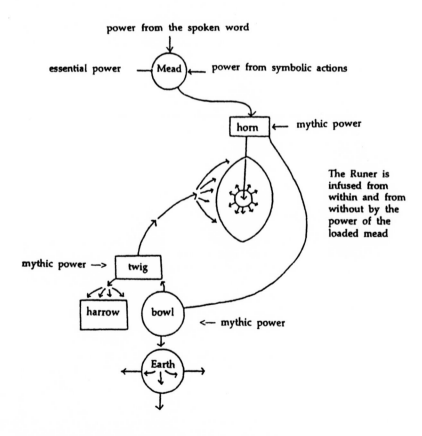

Figure 6.3: The Hidden Process of the Blessing

There are nine steps in the formula of the ritual blessing:

Name	Function
1) Hallowing	Sets ritual space/time apart from ordinary
2) Reading	Puts rite into a mytho-magical context
3) Rede	Links myth to purpose of the rite
4) Call	Invokes wights (gods or other entities)
5) Loading	Charges drink with power
6) Drinking	Circulates power within
7) Blessing	Circulates power without
8) Giving	Sends part of power to the invoked entity
9) Leaving	Declares the work done/return to ordinary

This formula can be used to form your own rites. An example of such a working is presented here as a blessing to the dwarf Alvíss (All-Wise). Lore about this dwarf can be learned from the "Alvíssmál" in the *Poetic Edda*. In writing your own versions the sections dealing with lore specific to the kind of wight being invoked will have to be composed.

To begin any complex working of this kind, you might want to empower yourself through Hammer- and Yew-Workings before beginning the rite as such— in such a case you will say the words of the Hallowing after completing these preliminary workings.

A Blessing to Alvíss
1) Hallowing
Perform a Hammer- Hail- or *Elhaz*-Working. Then say:
I HALLOW THIS HARROW TO THE WISDOM OF ALVÍSS. THROUGH THE MIGHT AND MAIN OF THE DEEP HALLS OF THE EARTH THIS STEAD IS WARDED.

2) Reading
Read the "Alvíssmál" from the *Poetic Edda*. After which sink into a period of silent meditation on the meanings of the poem.

3) Rede
THE DWARF ALVÍSS KNOWS THE LORE OF ALL THE SEVEN REALMS OF BEING. WITH THIS BLESSING I OPEN MY MIND AND MY HEART TO THE KNOWLEDGE AND WISDOM OF THESE SEVEN REALMS AS ALVÍSS WILL LEND ME THE LORE AND BEAR UP FROM THE DEPTHS OF HIS HALLS THE STAVES THAT I SEEK.

4) Call

ALL-WISE ONE, HEAR MY CALL! FROM THE DEPTHS OF DARKNESS IS THY LORE TO BE LEARNED. WEND THY WAY FORTH AND AS THY WAGE FOR THE WEAPONS OF WAR AND WISDOM A WIFE SHALL BE GIVEN. RISE UP ALVÍSS AND SPEAK THE STAVES THAT I SEEK.

5) Loading

The Runer pours the drink into the horn or other drinking vessel, holds it aloft in the right hand and says:

I BID THEE TAKE THIS MIGHTY GIFT OF BEER WHICH IS THY BRIDE! INTO THE DRINK I DRIVE DEALINGS OF MIGHT AND MAIN— RISING OUT OF THE DANK HALLS OF THY HOME AMONG THE DARK-ELVES. LET THIS HORN BE A SIGN OF THE EVERLASTING LINK BETWEEN THE REALMS BELOW AND THE KINGDOMS ABOVE— WHICH THOU KNOWEST SO WELL.

6) Drinking

The Runer makes the runic hand postures which spell the name Alvis(s) [A-L-W-I-S] above the rim of the horn and rowns the name into the liquid. (This concludes the loading process).

Now half of the liquid is drunk from the horn in three swallows.

7) Blessing

The rest of the of the liquid is poured out into the blessing bowl on the harrow. The liquid is stirred nine times with the evergreen sprig and the harrow and the Runer is sprinkled with the words:

THE WISDOM OF THE ALL-WISE ONE UPON ME AND THE WORLD!

8) Giving

The liquid is poured out of the blessing bowl onto the ground to the north of the harrow (or into the auxiliary bowl to the west of the harrow if the rite is performed indoors). As the liquid is poured the Runer says:

TO ALVÍSS— AND ALL THE DWARVES BELOW.

9) Leaving

In the ᛉ-staða, say:

THUS THE WORK HAS BEEN WROUGHT. THE WISDOM OF THE ALL-WISE HAS COME MY WAY.

Wight-Names

You will want to learn all about the various wights who can be called, dwarves, elves, etins, valkyries, and so forth. A sample of these and their meanings, which will determine what the aim of calling upon them would be is given here. A complete list would go into the hundreds.

A Selection of Dwarf-Names

Ái: The Great Ancestor (for knowledge of past existences)
Álf: The Shining One (Elf) (for the link between elves and
    dwarves)
Bláinn: The Black One (for secrets of the depths)
Dvalinn: One-Lying-In-Trance (for secrets of seið-work)
Nár: Corpse (for secrets of death)
Mjöðvitnir: Mead-Wolf (for motivation to knowledge)
Gandálfr: Magic-Elf (for secrets of magic of all kinds)
Þorinn: Bold One (for courage)
Fundinn: Found One (for finding things)
Nýi: New One (for renewal and rejuvenation)
Þekk: Pleasant One (for well-being)
Ráðsvið: Wise in Advice (for knowledge)
Ginnar: Enticer (to attract good things)
Dáinn: Dead One (for secrets of the dead)
Andvari: Foresighted One (for knowledge of future)
Óri: Raging One (for venting anger)

A Selection of Valkyrie Names

Brynhildr: Breast-plate of Battle (for protection)
Geirdriful: Spear-Thrower (for progress)
Herfjötur: Army-Fetterer (for stopping enemies)
Hild: Battle (for courage)
Hlokk: Noise of battle (for courage)
Hrund: Striker (for ability)
Randgrið: Shield-Destroyer (for breaking defenses)
Rota: One who Causes Confusion (for overcoming enemies)
Sigrdrífa: Victory Driver (for success beyond life and
    death)

The Seventh Door of Midgard
— Opening —

The Sixth and Seventh Doors are closely attached to one another. The Sixth was a consolidation of many things that had gone before. This continues in the Seventh, but also new ground is broken.

Skills learned in the blessing-work will be extended to the invocation of the high gods and goddesses of the runic pantheon. However, this will begin to take up less time in your daily work, because the gods and goddesses of Asgard and Wane-Home appreciate quality over quantity as far as the gifts given to them is concerned.

The most important section of this Door is the introduction to the process of the creation of the Wode-Self (the construction of a "magical persona"). This aspect is essential to the evolution of your self into that of a true Runemaster. In this Door will be the well-spring of the coming together of the one who gives, the given, and that to which gifts are given.

Reading

Now would be a good time to read the titles contained in category 4 of the reading list, and perhaps review the historical material in *Rune-Might*.

Daily Work

You should conduct this Door, like all Doors V-IX for approximately 72 days. In this time you will basically continue with the patterns of daily work you set up for the Sixth Door, but the number of invocations to Wōden or Freyja should be kept to no more than twice a week. The skills developed in the Sixth Door are applied in an efficient and deeply felt way in the Seventh Door.

Blessing-Work II
Runic Uses of Invocation

Calls to the God and Goddess of the Gild

The ritual formula introduced in the Sixth Door can also be used to invoke and commune with the two principal divinities of the Gild, Wōden and Freyja. In practicing these rites the Runer will be gaining deeper levels of understanding about these two main divinities of the Gild and will also be able to use the power invoked with them to help load tines or do other forms of Rune-galdor. At this point in your runic development, you are quite well prepared to construct your own blessings of this kind based on the traditional formula given in the

Sixth Door. However, for the sake of completeness, an example of Blessings to Wōden and Freyja are given here. Do not perform these rites too often, for reasons noted above.

A Blessing to Wōden

1) Hallowing
Perform the Hail- or *Elhaz*-Working and say:
THIS STEAD IS HALLOWED — FILLED WITH MIGHT AND MAIN FLOWING FROM THE HALLS OF ASGARD — AND SUNDERED FROM THE WORLD OF MEN, MADE HOLY TO THE WORK OF THE WISE.

2) Reading
The *"Rúnatals þáttr Óðins"* ("Hávamál" 138-165) in the *Poetic Edda*.

3) Rede
I DO NOT COME TO WORSHIP Wōden BUT TO LEARN HIS WAYS. IT IS MY HIDDEN WILL TO WEND MY WAY ALONG THE PATHWAYS OF SLEIPNIR, TO LISTEN TO THE LORE ROWNED BY HUGINN AND MUNINN, TO FEED THE HUNGER OF THE FRIENDLY WOLVES. I SIT IN THE HALL OF Wōden HIGH IN ASGARD AND COME TO KNOW HIS WAYS.

4) Call
OUT OF THE HORNS OF HEAVEN ALL-EIGHT I CALL TO THE O ELDEST OF THE GODS! I CALL THEE FROM ATOP THE TREE OF THE WORLD TO FARE FORTH TO US FROM THY HIGH SEAT HLIÞSKJALF.

5) Loading
The Runer pours the drink into the horn or other drinking vessel, holds it aloft in the right hand and says:
MAKE THY WAY INTO THIS DRINK O MIGHTY GALDOR-FATHER AND GIVER OF VICTORY. FILL THIS MEAD WITH THY MIGHT AND MAIN, AND BLEND IT WITH THY BOONS OF WISDOM.

6) Drinking
The Runer makes the runic hand postures which spell the name Wōðanaz
[W-O-Þ-A-N-A-Z] above the rim of the horn and rowns the name into the liquid. (This concludes the loading process).
Now half of the liquid is drunk from the horn in three swallows.

7) Blessing
The rest of the of the liquid is poured out into the blessing bowl on the harrow. The liquid is stirred nine times with the evergreen sprig and the harrow and the Runer are sprinkled with the words:
THE BLESSINGS OF ALL-FATHER UPON ME!

8) Giving
The liquid is poured out of the blessing bowl onto the ground to the north of the harrow (or into the auxiliary bowl to the west of the harrow if the rite is performed indoors). As the liquid is poured the Runer says:
TO Wōden THE GALDOR-FATHER AND GIVER OF GOOD SPEED!

9) Leaving
In the Y-staða, say:
NOW THE WORK OF Wōden HAS BEEN WROUGHT, AND I WEND MY WAY FORTH IN WISDOM AND WEAL! Wōden, HAIL! WASSAIL!

A Blessing to Freyja

1) Hallowing
Perform the Hail- or *Elhaz*-Working and say:
THIS STEAD IS HALLOWED — FILLED WITH MIGHT AND MAIN FLOWING FROM THE HALLS OF FOLKVANG IN VANAHEIM— AND SUNDERED FROM THE WORLD OF MEN, MADE HOLY TO THE WORK OF THE WISE.

2) Reading
Read or recite the "Hynduljóð" in the *Poetic Edda*.

3) Rede
I AM COME TO THIS STEAD TO HONOR Freyja. TO SPEAK OF MY LUSTS FOR HER LOVELY BODY, AND OF MY GREED FOR HER MIGHTY POWERS OF SEIÞ. WITH THESE WORDS I WISH WITH ALL MY HEART SHE WILL COME TO ME TO BE WITH ME IN BODY AND SOUL.

4) Call
I CALL TO THEE TO COME FARING OUT OF FOLKVANG AND FROM THY SEAT AT SESSRUMNIR— TO BE HERE WITH ME NOW. STRIDE FORTH IN THY GUISE AS GULLVEIG — THE ONE WHO THIRSTS FOR GOLD — AND MAKE THY HOLY MIGHT KNOWN IN THE SHAPE OF HEIÞ— THE SHINING BRIGHT MOTHER OF MIGHTY SEIÞ!

5) Loading
The Runer pours the drink into the horn or other drinking vessel, holds it aloft in the right hand and says:
MAKE THY WAY INTO THIS DRINK O TEACHER OF SEIÞ AND THE CRAFT OF SOOTH-SAYING. FILL THIS MEAD WITH THY MIGHT AND MAIN, AND BLEND IT WITH THY FAIRNESS AND FROLIC.

6) Drinking
The Runer makes the runic hand postures which spell the name Fraujōn [F-R-A-U-J-O-N] above the rim of the horn and rowns the name into the liquid. (This concludes the loading process).
Now half of the liquid is drunk from the horn in three swallows.

7) Blessing
The rest of the of the liquid is poured out into the blessing bowl on the harrow. The liquid is stirred nine times with the evergreen sprig and the harrow and the Runer are sprinkled with the words:
BLESSINGS OF THE LADY ALL-BRIGHT UPON ME AND UPON THE WORLD!

8) Giving
The liquid is poured out of the blessing bowl onto the ground to the north of the harrow (or into the auxiliary bowl to the west of the harrow if the rite is performed indoors). As the liquid is poured the Runer says:
TAKE WELL WITH THIS, MY GIFT TO THEE, QUEEN OF HEAVEN AND LADY ON-HIGH!

9) Leaving
In the Y-staða, say:
NOW MY WORK IN HONOR OF THE LADY IS WROUGHT. LET HER WEND HER WAY BACK TO THE WEST AND RETURN IN LOVE TO HER MANY-SEATED HALL UPON THE FEARSOME PLAIN HIGHT FOLKVANG.

It should be remembered that generally the attitude of the male Runer is that he imitates or emulates Wōden as an archetypal or exemplary model for his consciousness or behavior, while if he is going to worship any thing in the usual sense of giving his honor, love and devotion to something seen as essentially outside himself, a goddess, usually Freyja or some other feminine entity will be the recipient of this attention. For female Runers, the situation is reversed.

In days of yore, and today as well, there are Runers who do not "believe in" the gods and goddesses at all— but only trust in their own might and main, that is their own internal powers as derived from the original intellectual and spiritual gifts imparted by the threefold essence of Wōden. This is a very valid approach to the Odian path, but even these may on occasion choose to exercise the power contained in such rituals or modeling of reality because it is "most convenient."

The Work of the Wode-Self
(Construction of the "Magical Persona")
Part I

Germanic magic in general and Rune magic in particular is a magic worked directly by a self-conscious magician. To make this kind of magic work to its maximal level of effectiveness the magician must work on elevating the over all power of his or her own self, and develop the ability to push that self into a state of hyper-consciousness in which it becomes analogous to a divinity. Only in this state can the Runer truly work in the Way of Wōden. These principles are already well-known to most Runers by now. But in this section of the Seventh Door we will begin to explore the technical methods of constructing and assuming a magical persona, or a magical ego-consciousness in which to work.

The basic concept here is among the oldest in Rune magic. The Runers are to raise their consciousness to a level of divinity (analogous to that of Wōden) so that they can truly work in imitation of the God. When the Runers of today carve the Runes, in so doing they are working in the divine pattern first laid out by the archetypal actions of Wōden:

> Runes wilt thou find,   and rightly read,
>> of wondrous weight,
>> of mighty magic,
>> which dyed the dread god,
>> which that made the holy hosts,
>> and were etched by Óðinn
>
>> ......
>
> thus did Óðinn write   ere the earth began
> when up he rose   in after time.
>> (Hávamál 143/145)

The psychological theory of how this aspect of Rune magic works is very clear in the traditional Germanic lore of the soul. (See *Runelore* pp. 167-173.) The normal ego-consciousness, the subjective I-focus of the self, is in or near the center of the soul (in or near the Midgard-center). Since this is where the magician normally lives, this is indeed the ideal center for this focus. However, when there is magic to be worked, this center can be shifted from the center to the apex of the soul— to the Asgard-center, if you will. This is the projection and assumption of the divine qualities of the self. In this state the magician acts as a god or goddess— divinity is not only realized here, it is actually exercised. This is in reality a higher ego-consciousness or re-focusing.

By now you have had a great deal of experience in re-focusing your awareness in the various wheels of the Yggdrasill structure within yourself. Therefore, this teaching concerning the methods for construction, realization, and exercise of the magical persona will be along a fairly easy pathway.

Historically this is the kind of magic recorded in some of the oldest runic inscriptions. The so-called Runemaster formulas may be as simple as the one found on the Bratsberg bow fibula (from around 500 CE) which reads **ek erilaz**, I, the Erulian. The meaning of such an inscription is most clearly seen in the theory of the Runemasters' assumption of a magical persona or god-form in order to do their work. This talismanic formula is the only visible manifestation of the ritual transformation that took place in order for a Runer, who lived almost 1500 years ago, to do his magical work. The actual carving of the Runes declaring his metamorphosis was a fundamental part of the ritual transformation itself. In carving the Runes declaring himself an Erulian, a "risen up," or ritually divinized self, he effected the transformation in imitation of Wōden's own divine actions.

It is important to realize that the Runer of old used a magical or initiatory name which acted as a focus or lens through which he projected his own self to a new realm of action. He did not assume the god-form of Wōden himself, but rather assumed his own unique and independent divine form. This is the most practical application of the idea that the Odian does not worship Wōden or Óðinn, but rather imitates his form. Wōden did not assume the image of a form "higher" than himself. He gave himself to himself (Hávamál 138) and the true Runer must ultimately follow him in this pathway.

To effect this complex working in a practical way the you must find or construct a magical name which will act as a focus for a fully developed magical persona and image. This form should be absolutely unique to yourself. To use objective god- or goddess-forms can be magically effective in the short term, but this does not end in the true Odian aim. You must then work on assuming this form in meditative and ritual work using a variety of runic techniques. Slowly but surely you will become more comfortable with your hyper-self, and will be able to work it more effectively.

The Building of the Runic Self

In reality you have been working toward this goal since the beginning of your work with the Runes and with the Nine Doors of Midgard. What has been partial up to now will now become complete.

In order to work in the way traditional to the true Erulian, the Runer must be able to create a magical entity within the self, focus on it, project consciousness into it, and work with it runically. It is a device with which the Runers are able to separate their every day consciousness from the physical body, leaving behind the limitations normally imposed upon them. This is a door-way to the work of shape-shifting, or projection of the hyde (ON *hamr*), known in standard Western occultism as "astral projection."

The first step in being able to do this reliably is to build up an alternate image of the self. This is keyed to certain ritual (working) symbols, such as a name (or names), a piece of ritual jewelry, a certain gesture, and so on.

You will build up an alternate physical image and an alternate mental or spiritual image as well. In this later work your original bright and murky lists from the PAD-Work and that whole part of your development can be brought to bear directly.

To build up an alternate physical image you may begin by using a large mirror in which you can see your entire body at once. In a detached meditative state look at yourself in the mirror as you would look at a stranger. Just fix the shape in your mind. Then close your eyes and reproduce the image in your mind's eye, just as you would with the visualization exercises in the First Door. A photograph of yourself may also be used to help in this process. The next step is to add movement to the image. Start with small movements and then go on to more involved ones. First observe yourself in the mirror, then move on to visualizing these movements in your mind's eye. You may further expand this exercise into other senses. Learn to "imagine" actively and vividly the feel of things, their smell, and so on. The next step in this exercise is optional. You may want to mentally re-configure your magical body image to one more symbolically in tune with your mental image you are creating at the same time. You may see yourself as the consummate heroic warrior in a Sigurd-type image, for example. What is important magically is that the image be rooted in reality, and that the mental and quasi-physical images be harmonious.

At the same time you are doing these exercises, you should be working on refining your mental image of yourself. Return to your lists of personal characteristics you did for the PAD-Work. From it, if you have not already, construct in your mind the ideal and unlimited persona — a virtual *Übermensch* — for yourself. This magical ideal should be maintained as a set of characteristics separate from your every day self for right now. This super-personality is not restricted by the limitations imposed on it by the world dominated by the minds of Loddfafners (non-initiates). This persona only needs the star map of the Runes to sail across and even reconfigure the waves of the wider worlds.

As a part of the construction of the mental ideal, you should chose a magical name at this time, if you have not done so already. This may take some research on your part. But it will be instructive and useful in practical magical ways as well. This magical name should reinforce the physical and mental images you are constructing. (Members of the Rune-Gild can get help from a Master of the Gild in this endeavor.)

At the conclusion of these exercises, which should take no more than three or four weeks to complete, you will have constructed an ideal magical image both quasi-physical and spiritual (a sort of unlimited magical personality).

Yew-Work VI

The next step in the Yew-Work is the activation of the full array of the orb, Rune-ring, and the inner net-work of worlds and road-ways. By now it is clear that what you have been undergoing in this work is nothing less than the initiatory process of Óðinn's Self-Sacrifice on the World-Tree. Until now, in many ways, you have been hanging on the tree— now it is time to "fall back again" to return to the world to work your transformed will upon the very warp and woof of this world.

You have created and realized — at least in an embryonic or seed state — a microcosmic tree in your subjective world. This tree has direct links to the macrocosmic tree— you have learned the runic (hidden) language of the world now. You can speak to it, and it will respond to you. But remember, this is only the beginning of a long journey. Many refinements must be made before direct exercise of your might and main can be expected. Remember also that the doom of the gods is always neigh.

To activate the full potential of the Yew-Work, you first invoke all of the Runes of the objective world to presence in the Rune-band around you. Then you raise the Yew-column, and then do the Mill-Work to raise the available power to even higher levels, and finally do the Road-Work. If your work with the individual road-ways has been thorough, you will not have to spend time on each individual path before the entire network of "roots and branches" will be activated inside your personal sphere. Once this complete framework has been established, you can begin to experience the interlace or interweaving of the inner and outer worlds on a wholly new level. To begin doing this, sing the whole fuþark row of Rune names and with the singing of each of the names, see the power (in the form of a red fluid substance) flow from your center (in the Midgard-wheel) to the branch or root of Yggdrasill that you have identified with that Rune, and from there to the corresponding Rune in the Rune band. From that place in the objective world, it will return along its same path as you inhale for the singing of the next Rune name. This defines the full inner work for practices that you have been doing on a more superficial level for some time now.

The pathways along which the power is seen to flow can be visualized as either the roots and branches of the tree lying outside your body but inside your personal sphere, or they can be visualized in terms of the "runic physiology" outlined in the Fifth Door. In the case of using the runic physiology, the power will be seen to exit through the hands or feet to enter into the objective world and then back again.

Skills experienced and gained through the perfection of the Yew-Work are directly transferable to work in every other form of runic magic. Experience gained here will also give direct knowledge of why certain things are done in the accounts of old Germanic magic or why certain features are found repeatedly in Germanic artistic iconography— such as the interlace motif or the Rune-band serpents.

Galdor V

Now that you have mastered the working of the most ancient galdor formulas and felt their power, it is time to take that experience and extend it, along with the other Rune-knowledge you have gained, into the shaping of personalized Rune-galdors. In many ways the creation of a unique galdor is very much like the shaping of a specialized bind-Rune. Only instead of the medium of space, you use the medium of sound.

All media of working are usually combined in final workings. But any one of them might be able to effect the alterations or transformations that you desire. This is why it is so important to explore all of the ways of practicing Rune magic both in isolation and in combination with other methods.

After completion of this phase of galdor practice, the Runer should be able to shape any kind of galdor he or she wishes. Furthermore, you will have experienced the breadth and depth of the creation of galdor formulas, so that the analysis or reading of galdor created by others— whether they come from ancient Runemasters or modern ones.

In the exercise of creating you rown galdor formulas, you should start out with a basic but multifaceted idea or magical aim. Let us say you wish to have a unique Rune-song that will lend balanced magical and creative inspiration to you. You would first determine which Runestaves or traditional Rune-galdor you want to use to effect this end. I would choose the traditional formula *alu* along with the Runestaves for the K-Rune (for creativity) and the T-Rune (for balance as well as success). I might also add the Y-Rune (*elhaz*), if I wanted to reinforce the fact that my inspiration was to come from the gods and be connected to them. I might have also selected the A-Rune and the U-

Rune for their important qualities, but as they are already contained in the *alu*-formula, they are not to be repeated.

Out of this complex of ideas, and the array of Runestaves, I can not set about creating a harmonious galdor formula. The usual pattern for this is to start with the whole formula, the synthesized whole, and then go to an analysis of the whole — break it down into its component parts — and then re-integrate the whole anew. In the magical realm this is the equivalent of "creating," or more accurately, (re)-shaping the set of concepts you have combined in your galdor. In combining these things (perhaps for the first time in the exact form you have fashioned) you will be bringing the power of this combination into being for the first time. In the bloom of new creation there is great power. When you sing the song, you will be in the vortex of that power.

In the example start off with the singing of a combined, almost undifferentiated song:

   taaaaalllllkuuuuuuzzzzzz

Then sing the names of each of the individual Runes in isolation, combined with the traditional elemental formula, *alu*:

   tiwaz-ansuz-laguz-uruz-elhaz : alu

Then combine all of these elements into a final whole:

   alu : taaaalllllkuuuuuzzzzz : alu

This formula can be sung as many times as you wish. It can be used as a sort of sound-talisman — which is what galdors really are — to be sunk deep into your mind and memory where it can do its work throughout the worlds— within you and without you.

Staða-Work VII
Operative *Staðagaldr*

In *Futhark* (pp. 128-132) I presented several rites of *staðagaldr* adapted from the *Armanen* tradition. These could now more profitably be experimented with. The Runer is always free to add more complex verbal formulas to what is either said or thought while actually performing the Rune-standing. Precise verbal formulas in plain language help to focus the will more exactly.

Here as in all outer or technical aspects of Rune magic the Runer is encouraged to experiment widely. This is to find out what the most effective methods of working for you personally are. Such experimentation is especially important at this stage, as you will have built up more than enough technical expertise to do this effectively if you have followed the course of the Nine Doors up to now.

Perform the rites of *staðagaldr* as outlined in *Futhark* and record the results in your Galdor-Book.

Now with what you have learned of the practice of *staðagaldr* you are fully prepared to create your own rites for your own purpose, and to do this reliably and effectively. The runic formulas you might use would largely be the same as those you would use to create a *taufr* formula. The only additional element might be the creation of specific verbal formulas in natural language to reinforce the effects of the Rune-standings and the galdors that are sung while in these postures.

Example of a Creative *Staðagaldr* Formula

Let us suppose you want to create a formula of *staðagaldr* which will help you to uncover secret lore within yourself and within the books that you are reading. This secret lore is to be relevant to what you personally need to continue your progress right now. With this motive, a Runer might create a runic formula made up of the A- G- N- J- EI- P- Z- S- B- M- L- NG-Runes. The reasons for choosing these rues are made clear in the natural language formulas attached to each of them below.

Once you have your chosen Runes, you then arrange them in such a way as to illustrate your willed purpose most clearly. Next, you create one or two line formulas for each. These will focus and direct your thoughts after you have sung the runic galdor in the corresponding Rune-standing. You can speak the verbal formulas out loud, or you can just think them in your head— the effects will be the same.

After performing whatever ritual preparations seem necessary to you at this time, the Hammer-Working, Hail-Working, Yew-Working, etc. You might stand in the center of your ring and perform the sequence of Rune-standings by striking the posture and while in that posture singing the galdor of the Rune. After you have sung the galdor, speak or think the verbal loading or affirmation. For this example working the verbal formulas might be:

A-	Wisdom of the Ases, awaken
M-	Awaken the sleeping god(dess) within
N-	I do need this knowledge now.
G-	I shall get the gifts that are given
L-	I can pass all tests thrown my way
J-	Rightly have I worked, now come rewards
EI-	From above and below, I welcome wisdom
P-	By chance and wyrd may wisdom come
Z-	I am linked to the highest of life
S-	I aim for lore deep in my soul
B-	What was buried is now borne up
NG-	The seed of knowledge grows within

Probably the most important pragmatic aspect of the creation of such verbal formulas is that they be in language that speaks to your unconscious mind. The words and expressions used should be ones that are deeply meaningful to you. At the same time they must be short and to the point with no extra words.

This concludes the formal instruction on *staðagaldr*. In the final analysis, this form of magic is one which can incorporate a full integration of body-mind technique for magical purposes. However, if you are not particularly inspired by this technique, it can easily be left out of your development form here on.

Rune-Thinking VII

With this Door we will conclude with the formal aspects of training in Rune-thinking. However, these basics learned up to now should be repeated regularly, and you should now go on to innovate new and personalized methods of Rune-thinking to suit your own magical needs.

After you have worked your way through the many natural runic combinations of two and three Runes, you will have come to the point where you can spend some time on combinations you are attracted to for reasons that may have no direct natural explanation in the structure of the Fuþark. Choose two or three Runes to combine in your contemplative mood and explore their combined meaning(s). One way to pick such Runes is to look for those that are related in some outer form: for example from among the Þ-, R-, W-, P-, or B-Runes. You may even pick two or three Runes at random from your divinatory lots and contemplate the implications of their combined meaning. This sort of exercise is common in learning to read the Runes for divinatory purposes, but this is something different. You are not looking at what the runic combination might mean to you or to someone else in a divinatory sense, but rather you are looking at what the combination means in and of itself. You are looking for objective not subjective meanings now.

This is the beginning of a work that will end with your sudden and complete understanding of the entire **Fuþark** as one "word" which encompasses whole order of all the worlds.

This kind of contemplation of bind-Runes is done in exactly the same way as you did with the other runic combinations in the Sixth Door. Work on each combination of Runes until you feel that you have understood it in some essential way. Again record all results in the Galdor-Book.

As an auxiliary to this kind of work the Runer can undertake the contemplation of holy signs and *galdrastafir*. Holy signs and symbols such as the Irminsûl, the Hammer of Þórr, the sun-wheel, etc. can be contemplated for the Runes that they seem to contain or imply in their forms. Also, you can begin to try to understand and decipher the complex *galdrastafir*, such as the ones shown in *The Galdrabók* (Weiser, 1989).

This kind of Rune-thinking is best done in an unhurried way. Spend as much time as you need or want on each runic combination. Some may speak volumes to you, others may be relatively silent. This may be because the combination is simple, or because you have not developed the sense necessary to hear its message. Give them time to speak to you.

Taufr IV

In essence there is little difference between the techniques of signing and sending and risting the Runes. In the first the staves are "carved" in the air, while in the latter they are carved directly into physical media. Things you have learned about signing and sending can be applied to *taufr*, and the reverse is also true.

As an added magical technique you might want to have the capability of drawing runic powers from the Rune-ring (symbolizing the Runes of the objective universe) directly into your runic talisman. To do this, visualize a beam of red light (something like a laser might produce) streaming from the Rune-stave in its location in the Rune-ring right into the Rune-stave as you are carving it. You might even combine the flows of force— one coming from within, one coming from without meeting in the middle to shape a new entity. The power of this formula is unmistakable— as is the origin of the tradition in the basic Germanic idea of things being created in the meeting ground between to extremes.

Advanced Rune-Fastening Technique

The metaphysic of Germanic naming practices holds the key to an advanced technique of holding a runic charge on a talisman. In the Germanic Troth when a child is born it is sprinkled with water and given a name in a ritual setting. It is also given a gift which is said to have the effect of "fastening" the name to the body and soul of the child. In Old Norse this gift is called the *nafnfestr* (name-fastening). By the same token the Runer can help to fasten the Rune loading to a talismanic creature through the bestowing of a gift upon the *taufr*.

Since the *taufr* is a creature of runic power, gifts to it should come in this form. The best way to give the talisman such gifts is by means of a sacrificial blessing (ON *blót*). Using the blessing formula first given in the Sixth Door, construct a ritual blessing in which the *taufr* could be said to be the wight being honored or "worshipped." The offering given to the *taufr* should be in harmony with its magical purpose. If it is a *taufr* for inspiration it should get mead, if one for prosperity it should get grain or even coins (which you will bury in the earth).

This gift will fasten and fix the name and active capacity of the *taufr*, giving shape and direction to its life and *ørlög*.

Remember that once such a talisman has fulfilled its mission in life it is to be sent back to the Rune realms with all due ritual forms of respect. In a way, you will be performing a funeral rite for it when you burn or bury it in the earth to be reabsorbed into the objective universe.

The Eighth Door of Midgard
— Opening —

In the Eighth Door many of the things that you have been preparing for become manifest. You begin to move in the Rune realms with a new level of inner being. In addition, you will receive wholly new ways of working in the form of seið (ON *seið[r]*). You will have strengthened your sense of self to such an extent that the work in seið, which involves a loss of conscious control of your inner world, will be most gainfully undertaken. If the Runer engages too early or too deeply in seið-work (which can *roughly* be equated with shamanism) there could be an overall detriment in his or her runic development. That is not to say that seið is in any overall sense "dangerous," it is just not recommended to those whose primary interest is in the field of Odian development of the self.

Reading

Wiccan Sex-Magic, Inga Steddinger
A Source Book of Seið, S. E. Flowers and J. A. Chisholm
Witchdom of the True, Edred

At this time also review any works that you have neglected over the course of the other Doors. Also, the work *The Way of the Shaman* by Michael Harner may be found valuable for those with a special interest in seið-work at this time.

— Daily Work —

This Door should take about 72 days to complete. The main daily work you will be doing at this time involves the regular practice of the basic techniques of seið. This should be strongly balanced with the regular and frequent entry into the state of the Wode-Self, the magical persona, in which you become aware to a hyper-degree of the almost god-like character of this aspect of the self.

During the time of this Door, go into the state of the Wode-Self at least every three days or so, even if it is just for the experience of its power and to gain knowledge of its character. This will only increase the power and effectiveness of every other kind of work you do.

Building of the Wode-Self
Construction of the Magical Persona
Part II

The next step in this basic runic process is the unification of the every day self with the self-created quasi-physical and mental bodies for magical purposes. The idealized forms are steps along the pathway for you to assume a god- or goddess-like status analogous to that of Wōden or Freyja.

First, in a ritual setting, in the context of the fully activated magical ring (in the Yew-Working), consciously meld the quasi-physical image with the idealized mental persona in a form standing in front of you in the Y-Rune posture facing in the same direction about one foot away. Once the image is fully evoked in your mind's eye, step into it with the words:

I, (magical name)!

As you step forward smoothly meld your body with that of the idealized images as you glide into the Y-Rune posture yourself. You and the ideal are become one.

This is your basic symbolic link among these three aspects of yourself. Remember that all three aspects are indeed parts of your greater, at least in potentiality, integrated and whole self. At this point all three aspects are unified and congruent with your physical body (lyke).

The working of bringing these aspects together can be expanded and modified. For example, it can include the donning of a particular piece of jewelry (which you would only wear when in this integrated state). Ideally the working will consist first and foremost of the speaking of the formula: "I (+ your magical name)." This verbal action is accompanied by the magical gesture of going into the Y-Rune posture. It might also be advisable to compound this gesture with hand postures that are unique to this operation so that the Y-Rune exercise will not be totally identified with this operation— even though this transformational link is fundamental to the very mystery of that Rune-stave.

Every formal entry into the magical persona, or Wod-I (inspired ego-consciousness) should be ended with a formal gesture, such as the assumption of the D-Rune posture as you mentally and/or physically step back from the idealized persona and image.

The building and assumption of this divinized form of the self is one of the most basic aspects of the magic of the Erulians. In this state you are most truly imitating the state of being you share with the god Wōden or the goddess Freyja. In this state you do your most effective work. In this state even the speaking of formulas will have magical effect in your subjective universe, and the risting of the Runes of formulas will have direct effect on the objective universe. This the key to the understanding of many of the inscriptions left behind by our predecessor Erulians. The mysteries of this process are further explored by the Fellows and Masters of the Gild.

Road-Wending I
Runic Journeys through the Worlds

Looking at the cosmological scheme presented in Door III, you will see that there are 9 worlds or realms of being, and that these are connected by 24 paths or road-ways. In reality, this is only the most exterior of a vast array of complex realms and interconnections of them, all alluded to the Eddic literature, where we read of many halls and realms, and many paths, rivers and streams leading from and to them. The only way to make sense of these mysteries is to experience them.

In runic road-wending the Runer will learn to make the Journeys between and among the various worlds in order to learn directly about the Runes (mysteries) connecting these realms. What you have already learned of the lore of the Runes will be the key to your explorations of these realms. But in exploring them you will also add to your direct runic knowledge in ways that can not be learned from human teachers or from books.

The myths found in the *Poetic* and *Prose Eddas* about gods and other beings traveling from one realm to another show that this kind of lore was very wide-spread in the ancient tradition. One of the reasons why you have so constantly been urged to read and absorb the mythology contained in these texts is that it will act as an objective (yet often extremely subtle) guide to the explorations of the realms of Yggdrasill.

Road-wending is very much like the shamanistic practices of seið, but whereas in the working of seið the Runer will aim for a loss of conscious control over what he or she is seeing or hearing, in the practice of road-wending, the objective monitors of the transpersonal tradition (whispered by Muninn) and of your personal intellect (whispered by Huginn) are always at your shoulders and never far away.

Step 1

To begin the practice of road-wending the Runer should consult the map of Yggdrasill provided in Door III, and meditate on the qualities of any two of the worlds. In doing this the Runer will synthesize the two qualities, and once a feel for this synthesis is developed, the Runestave most closely corresponding to that feeling should be at least provisionally ascribed to that pathway or road. You can spend several days doing this exercise, taking note of your results in the Galdor-Book.

Step 2

Now take a different Rune (and roadway) each day and contemplate the Rune-road. In doing this you will be bringing together what you know of the Rune, and of the two realms that the Rune connects (for you). In actuality each of the Rune-roads contains a complete Fuþark in its structure, however, at certain times and with certain Runers, one or another Rune may be felt to rule the road. There is an objective set of correspondences to the pattern, but knowledge of it is more detrimental than helpful at this stage. As you contemplate the road-way, let any images or symbols occur to you that come up, do not try to force any imagery, but keep the triangle of:

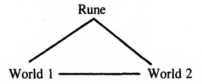

Rune

World 1 ———————— World 2

firmly in mind. The aim at this point is to establish a deeper feel for the complexity of each of the pathways. You should probably not consider your work complete until you have experienced each of the road-ways at least three times in this manner.

Seið-Work I
Seið in History

In the ancient North there were two different kinds of magic, galdor (ON *galdr*) and seið (ON *seiðr*). While galdor emphasizes the development of will and of conscious control of the self and of the environment (the subjective and objective universes) through analytical symbols of communication (Runes, galdor-staves, etc.), seið is more about the loss of control and the submerging of the self in something deep within or without the seið-man or woman. In many ways seið is the shamanism and the tantrism of the Germanic North. Technically, however, it is not shamanism. It is most probably this form of magic was the basis for the practice of *wiccecræft*, which is the Old English form of seið-work.

The saga tradition (*Ynglinga Saga*, ch. 7) tells us that it was the Vanic goddess Freyja who first taught the craft of seið to the Ases— and specifically to the Galdor-Father, Wōden. Seið is the magical art form of the Wanes, while galdor it that of the Ases. The Rune-Gild curriculum essentially stems from the Halls of Wōden and the Ases, however, the seið-craft was also a mainstay of the complete Odian curriculum in ancient times, and it should remain so today. It is something that best comes after thorough training in Runelore and Rune-work. By the same token, Freyja has certainly learned a great deal from the galdor of Wōden, and the two forms of magic can certainly be (re-)synthesized into a harmonious whole— from which they originally evolved.

Originally the forms of magic that came to be classified later as seið were probably the magical traditions cultivated in the so-called "third function" of the Indo-European culture and religion. This was the magic of the farmers and herdsmen, of the craftsmen and smiths, of the musicians and entertainers. Their magic was powerful and unique, and was probably dominated by female practitioners. As the Indo-

Europeans moved into Europe several millennia ago, this branch of their magic quickly became assimilated to the local forms of magic indigenous to the folk of Old Europe.

This is an area of the Germanic esoteric tradition which is not very copiously documented. In order to follow our usual process of working with material traditionally, we have to delve deeply into the sources for the practice of seið we do possess in order to extract the practical nuggets from the material. All references to the practice of seið have been collected and translated in a convenient edition: *A Source Book of Seið* (Rûna-Raven, 2002). One should be especially on guard when those claiming to practice seið are really enacting techniques borrowed from foreign sources without regard to what we do know about the practice of seið from our Germanic sources.

The runic system of the Odians (Erulians) took this kind of magic into account and learned it (hence the myth of Freyja teaching seið to Wōden). The runic system incorporated some of the doctrines and practices of seið into its structure, and it always formed a part of the curriculum of initiation into the runic mysteries.

In later Pagan times (that is in the so-called Viking Age) the practice of seið developed a reputation for being "shameful" or "unmanly." This probably stems from the fact that control was/is an important part of what it means to be virtuous or "manly" in the mind-set of the Heathen Germani. Since the practice of seið involves the loss of control— it came to be seen as "shameful." Another reason why this form of magic could be called "unmanly" is that it sometimes involved *ergi* (passive anal intercourse), but that was not prevalent enough to give this reputation to the whole school of magic.

The negative reputation of seið was a late development, to be sure, and probably one that shows the break-down of the true Heathen culture under pressure from socioeconomic pressures from the Christian south.

When the days of conversion to Christianity did finally come the craft of seið and the magic of Freyja was singled out for the harshest persecution. It is mainly for this reason that so little of the traditions of seið have survived.

What has survived is mainly that which took refuge in the Odian tradition. There it lived on until now it is in a position to be reborn in its own right.

Seið has many things in common with what is practiced as neo-shamanism. The recent upsurge in interest in the shamanism of exotic peoples may essentially be rooted in a remanifestation of similar interests inherited from our own ancestors. If this is the case, then it might be a good idea for us to investigate our own ancestral forms of magic — to seek within — before running off to find an exotic solution.

In theory traditional seið rests on three pillars:

    1) trance (loss of conscious control of mental
           processes)

    2) slumber (loss or radical alteration of data
           coming in through the physical
           senses— sleep of the body)

    3) rhythm (use of a rhythmic beat to "ride" while
           doing seið-work.)

Certain actual techniques of seið will make more use of these features than others. There is really a whole culture of seið-work waiting to be re-awakened— a magical culture that includes forms of song, dance, symbolism, ritual, and religion. But that is not our purpose here.

At this time the Runer will see why the blessings of Freyja might have been so important— in asking her to teach you the craft of seið. Her help will prove invaluable in the lessons you will learn directly from her and her friends.

In this Door we will cover exercises in the three basic forms of seið-craft:

    1) sooth-saying (divination)
    2) faring forth (traveling in other realms)
    3) love-seið   (sex magic)

The first two of these will be outlined under the heading of basic seið-work and will not be distinguished for in this program. The major use for faring forth into other realms will be sooth-saying.

Basic Seið-Work

One of the three basic areas of seið-work is sooth-saying, which is just an archaic way of saying "truth-telling." This is a traditional form of divination or clairvoyance practiced from the most archaic times.

Sooth-saying is very different from divination by Runecasting because in that craft, the analytical part of the mind is used to gain access to the whole realm beyond (in good galdor tradition), whereas with sooth-saying a more direct mode of access to actual beings or entities beyond the rational mind is attempted directly. Interaction with the beings known as dises, norns, valkyries, or dwarves, elves, or etins is extremely ancient among the Germanic peoples.

Belief in these beings certainly has one of its roots in the cult of Germanic ancestor worship, and another root in the lore of the demigods who were attached to certain great or powerful persons, or were the entities responsible for assisting in the teaching of arcane crafts— from galdor and seið to the crafts of smithing and singing. Because of these links, it is easy to see some kind of connection between what goes on in seið-craft and what was called "spiritualism" in a former time, more popularly known as "channeling" today. Indeed, there are connections— but the transpersonal, ancient and internally coherent lore and work of the Germanic tradition gives the practitioner much more solid pathways to go on than does the often confused modern practice.

One of the best examples of this kind of sooth-saying is given in the *Saga of Erik the Red* (chapter 4), but hints and references to this kind of seið-craft is found in many places in Icelandic literature.

To induce the trance-like state in which you can "say sooth" there are several things to do. First you must be able to get into a state of thought vacuum (see Door I)— relax your body totally. Relax your body part by part, working from your feet all the way up to the top of your head. Visualize yourself in a sphere of gentle reddish pink light. The over all effect should be one of relaxation, but on a deep down level it should be invigorating and vivifying.

After practicing this a few times, renew some exercises in concentrating your will— this time on sounds— rhythms and other effects of sound. In this you may want to have a recording of music or simple rhythms to assist you. The book *The Way of the Shaman* by Michael Harner has some practical suggestions worthy of consideration. **Do not rely too heavily on the ideas in this book, however, as the Germanic tradition is significantly different from the ones used as theoretical examples in Harner's methods.** It should especially be noted that the ancient Germanic "shamans" did not use drums— they seem to have produced the same or similar effects through the rhythmic chanting of their assistants or by rhythmic striking upon a wooden shrine.

The next step is designed to help open the doors between the seið-man or woman and the natural world— to bring the Runer into tune with natural things outside his or her consciousness. To do this, the Runer should gather six things— three from the mineral world (for example a loadstone, a quartz crystal, and a piece of granite), and three from the vegetable world (for example a branch of evergreen, an acorn, and a leek). When in your receptive, relaxed state, feel these objects— let your mind enter into them and meld with them. Concentrate on breaking down the barrier between yourself and these substances. Note how each feels and how each feels different in your Galdor-Book.

At this point, if not before, the Runer will have recognized that this kind of magic is something qualitatively different from that which he or she has been practicing in the Nine Doors up until now. In the galdor-work the emphasis has been on the strengthening of the will and of the sense of self as something essentially separate from the environment at large. This approach is the hard-headed and realistic view dominant in Rune-galdor, but the crafts of seið are also important to the ultimate development of the Runer. No experience is to be shunned.

Next, you should work for a while getting your body in a completely relaxed state. This should be so deep that it seems that you no longer have any of the five senses. (Modern technology provides sensory deprivation tanks that can bring the seið-woman to this state quickly.) One of the ancient techniques was to cover the head with a hood— really a kind of bag or sack which covered the whole head. This may have also regulated the intake of oxygen such that a trance state was more easily achieved also. (In this regard, it might be noted that in ancient times the on-set of a yawning fit was a sure sign that the seið-man was about to enter a seið-slumber.)

Once you are satisfied with the level of "trance" or seið-slumber you are able to achieve, let the stream of thought open between your conscious mind (hugh) and the receptive mind (myne). It should be as if the myne were a reflecting pool for states of being beyond your realm (Midgard). Let the myne reflect from above, below and all around. Your work with road-wending will be of indirect help here. Spend one day allowing the myne to reflect from one direction, and another day from another direction. Feel which realm you have the greatest affinity for at this time— is it Etin-Home, Dwarf-Home, or Elf-Home? Spend most of your time reflecting in that direction. Concentrate on the ability to make conscious the things that are received by the myne.

Now actually allow yourself to feel as if you were either ascending to Elf-Home above, or descending into Dwarf-Home below, or going out into Etin-Home. Do not think that "sinking down" into Dwarf-Home is in any way dangerous or "negative," or in any way more dangerous than any of the other destinations. There are lessons to be learned and experiences to be had in every direction. (Note that neo-shamanistic practices usually involve the descent of the shaman, while modern "channeling" usually has the channeler ascend to do the work. Seið-work is multi-directional and realizes the benefits to be gained from all the worlds.)

By this time you have been quite well trained in the exploration of your own self and your own tradition that you can critically study and use the literature of neo-shamanism and channeling with benefit.

This last part of the exercise is what is known as "faring forth" into other realms for purposes of seið. In this exercise we are only using this technique for sooth-saying, however, it can be used for a variety of operative ends for those who delve deeply enough.

The last exercise in sooth-saying for this Door will be to allow yourself to "speak" to some entity in the other realm, and to report what it, he, or she says in Midgard.

To do this, you allow yourself to rise higher and higher into Elf-Home, or to descend lower and lower into Dwarf-Home, or to go farther and farther out into Etin-Home, or to journey in some other way to one of the other realms that you have learned about in the lore of the worlds.

Once you find yourself at a certain place in that world, a door, gate, cave opening, or some other kind of entry way will present itself to your mind's eye. At the same time, beings in that world will approach you. See them, interact with them, attempt some form of communication. They may or may not be able to communicate with you verbally. It is more likely that images, sounds and feelings will pass between you.

If one of these beings presents itself as your warden (guardian) make friends with it. Exchange gifts of love and fellowship with it, try to find out its name if you can. At this time you may with to return to Midgard, but if you feel very strong and drawn to do so, enter through the door or other opening before you in the company of your warden.

Ask your warden questions, let it respond to you and try to communicate these in Midgard. (Leaving a tape recorder on in the room if you are working alone is a good idea in these exercises.) In this way you will be practicing the most basic form of true sooth-saying.

Another form of sooth-saying can be worked with the help of a bowl (the blessing bowl can be used for this, but you might want to have one especially given to this purpose). The bowl should be about two inches deep and at least six or seven inches in diameter. Most traditionally it will be made out of ash wood. Put water in the bowl and strew some herbal yarrow in the water. When in the receptive state gaze into the water and allow images to rise up. As these do so, communicate them verbally.

A note might be added about the word warden. In English we have the word warlock which comes from the Old Norse term *varðlokkur* meaning songs (*lokkur*) to attract the *vörðr* (guardian, warden-spirit). Then this word became attached to those who sang these *lokkur* or practiced the craft of attracting and communicating with these *varðar*. This work is deeply rooted in our tradition.

These exercises are valuable in themselves as ways to open yourself to the work of sooth-saying. But they are also valuable as preparation for the work of "sitting out" (ON *útiseta*) which we will see in the next and last Door.

Love-Seið

This kind of seið is something that some Runers may elect to forgo. It is not for everyone, and besides it is something that lies outside the technical field of operative runology in that Runestaves *per se* are not necessary to its practice. However, in love-seið there are indeed great Runes to be discovered. Otherwise Wōden would not have sought out knowledge of it from the goddess of the Wanes, Freyja.

The idea of using sexual activity and symbolism of that activity in magic is probably as old as humanity. There is something intrinsically and universally powerful about human sexuality that goes far beyond its natural function of reproduction. In this, as in other even more obvious areas, humans exceed all other animals to an extent that must be called non-natural. The often times unusual aspects of human sexuality are further indications of the spiritual character of the species. The use of the power inherent in this aspect of the human heart and mind is often alluded to in the traditional sources of Germanic lore.

It is, however, a general mistake made by some enthusiasts to think that seið is first and foremost some form of "sexual magic." Seið *might* include sexual magic, but it is not defined sexually.

In the runic tradition itself this sexual component is referred to darkly in the "Hávamál" st. 164:

> That eighteenth I know   which I never make known,
>   to a maid or a man's wife—
> anything is better,   than if one knows it;
>   this belongs to the last of my lays—
> but only to the one   in whose arms I lie,
>   or else who is my sister.

Here Óðinn says that this ultimate sort of magic is not to be revealed to or practiced with virgins (non-initiates in sexuality) or to other men's wives, that it is a burden to have knowledge of it, that it is the "last" of the spells (that is, it is the ultimate or highest as recounted in the "Hávamál," and that it is to be revealed to a lover or a "sister." This sister may be interpreted as a biological sister (after all Freyja and Freyr were brother and sister but also lovers), or an initiatory sister— a fellow Runer.

This refers to magical knowledge and power being passed from the male initiate to the female (the reverse is also well known), and to the fact that this is an approach to the discovery of the Rune— the ultimate from which all the Runes are derived.

Typical in the mytho-magical tales of the North are those that show a magician spending one or several nights with a seið-woman, etin-wife, or other holder of magical power in order to earn a reward for his good company. The most important of these formulas is that of Wōden's rewinning of the poetic mead (*Prose Edda, Skáldskaparmál* ch. 2) where the god spends three nights with the etin-wife Gunnlöð to regain the mead of poetic inspiration. This whole myth can be given a sex-magical interpretation that will reveal great Runes.

One of the most remarkable kinds of sex magic depicted in the traditional Germanic sources is that of *ergi*, which involves anal intercourse. Through this method it is shown how certain magicians are able to cast powerful curses or create monstrous entities to do their malevolent bidding.

The traditional literature is full of veiled references to this kind of seið in many different forms. But these references are quite obscure and it is almost impossible to get a clear idea of any theory that the ancient Teutons might have had about this kind of seið.

It is clear that a form of auto-erotic magic was practiced as well as one involving another person. Most likely the auto-erotic practices reflect a theory of sexo-magical relations with the "lover within," the contra-sexual spiritual entity attached to the individual. This is at least one facet of the myths dealing with the love between a warrior and his valkyrie, for example that of Siguròr and Sigrdrífa (Brynhildr) in the "Sigrdrífumál" in the *Poetic Edda* or Helgi and Sváva/Sigrún/Kára in the Helgi Lays, also in the *Poetic Edda*.

The lover within can become the lover without. When this happens sexual magic can also be practiced between two independent human lovers. In such cases energy is exchanged as the two "trees" of the people intertwine and seið is practiced from the self-created fire kindled through sexual contact between two.

Love-seið is among the most complex and technically most multifaceted aspects of Germanic magic. In this Door only a superficial introduction can be offered. Its true exploration and mastery lies beyond these Nine Doors. At this stage the Runer is advised, if he or she feels inclined to try this kind of seið, to become familiar with the practice of sexual magic from a historical perspective and to begin pragmatic experiments in this area.

It should be remembered that it was the seið of Freyja and the lore of that kind of magic that was most vigorously suppressed by the church in the North. The legacy of that repression remains with us today. This means that dealing with matters that combine sexuality and magic are fraught with certain ethical questions, and with matters relating to the psychology of the individuals involved. Despite the widely held notion that we live in an age of sexual liberation, the fact is that we still have centuries of Christian programming to deal with before we can hope to get back to the attitudes that prevailed before the imposition of that exotic viewpoint on our ancestors.

Realizing the importance of all this is essential from a pragmatic standpoint. Because if these ideas are not dealt with now, they will only interfere at a later time.

Pragmatically the main thing about love-seið is that it works on the basis of sexual energy or arousal. The higher the level of sexual excitement the higher the level of "energy" available to the seið-man or woman.

When we observe the Germanic tradition, we see that when sexual magic is implied it is usually in the context of something that is normally forbidden or "tabu."

The central event in the working of love-seið is the orgasm (or the sublimation of it).

If we assume that any sensory object or event having its origin outside the will and consciousness of the Runer is potentially a magical tool (whether this is the sight of a Runestave, the feel of the rister in your hand, or the taste of the mead) then we must allow that the orgasm and sensations and events (subjective and objective) leading up to and triggering it are among the most powerful and universal available to the Runer.

The meaning of the orgasm has two stages: 1) It is an event in the lyke (body) and linked to an event in the soul both involving the build up and release of energy and tension. 2) It is thought to be a manifold magico-symbolic "substance" in the form of a powerful sensation. This like the substance used to redden the Runes and be formed in any shape and bent to any purpose willed by the Runer.

The exploration of the actual practice of love-seið begins with the exploration of the most powerful ways the power of Freyja can be raised in yourself. The more ways this can be done the better, the more intense the desires and arousal possible the better. Explore your own sexuality. Find its limits and borders. Doing this is one of the most pious and worshipful acts you can do in honor of the goddess Freyja.

Once this aspect of magical research has been explored sufficiently — which may have been virtually completed by imaginative sixteen year olds — then comes the practice of harnessing these forces to your will. This is done by manipulating the orgasm in as many ways as possible. Exercises such as coming to the brink of orgasm and retreating from that point many times is useful, as are others such as seeing how quickly orgasms can be reached, how many times it can be reached in various spans of time, refraining from sexual activity for certain pre-set lengths of time.

On the level of the inner world love-seið is closely bound up with finding and dealing with the fetch-lover within— the fetch or valkyrie. This lover is the counterpart to your own wode-self or magical persona. Your mundane, or lyke-self will act as an agent for bringing this lover together with your wode-self— eventually leading to a synthesis of all three.

You should begin to build up the ideal lover in your mind. This exercise follows closely the steps used to build up the wode-self or magical persona— which usually is of the same sex as your own physical body. The lover will usually be of the opposite sex. Create the ideal lover in all details— what does he or she look like, what character traits doe she or she have, and so on? Find out what his or her name is. In doing all this you are really discovering the slumbering secret lover within, not creating something out of nothing.

After you have identified the over and discovered the name, begin to bind the lover to you (more exactly to your wode-self). This is most often done through auto-erotic practices. If, however, you already have a steady relationship with a human person— you may begin to project (with that person's conscious cooperation) the divine lover-self onto that person during workings of love-seið. This is most effective if done in a mutual kind of activity.

All of this forms a powerful preliminary to the practice of the *útiseta* working in the last Door. However, it is not absolutely necessary to do love-seið in order to be able to carry out the work of *útiseta*.

A Note on Shape-Shifting

One of the most widespread uses of seið-craft in ancient times was the practice of shape-shifting. But it must be noted that there were also methods in galdor-craft that could achieve the same ends. Sometimes it is hard to tell which method is being used. We get a telling account of this practice in the *Ynglinga Saga* (chapter 7) where it says "Óðinn could shift his shape. When he did this his body would lie there as if it were in a slumber or dead— but he himself went at once to far off lands on his own errands or those of other men in the shape of a bird, animal, fish, or serpent." Here we see that the body would be in a state of suspended animation and the it was not the body itself which shifted its shape but rather another alternate "shape" (or hyde) was synthesized elsewhere. This shows a more sophisticated view of the process than many might have expected.

In some instances these alternate shapes were used for reconnaissance only, while the most famous examples tell of huge animal-shapes being formulated to do a seið-man's fighting for him. The only problem was that wounds inflicted on the alternate shape would manifest on the body of the sleeping seið-man.

The practice of shape-shifting is obviously one of the most advanced kinds of Germanic magic, and is beyond the scope of this format. However, it remains an outstanding example of the technical sophistication of the ancient theories of how this kind of seið or galdor worked.

The Ninth Door of Midgard
— Opening —

The Ninth Door is something quite different from all the other Doors that have gone before. The Ninth Door is a phase of synthesis and the expression of that synthesis in a communicable form. If the Runer has gotten this far working in the program now is the ideal time to make contact with the Rune-Gild and work the Ninth Door within a Hall of the Gild, and in consultation with a Rune-Master of the Gild.

Throughout the Nine Doors we have been practicing a certain method, almost unique to true Odianism— as we have oscillated back and forth in our work between the subjective/reflective world and the objective/cognitive worlds within us. We have, in Odian terms, turned our hears back and forth between Muninn and Huginn, to hear both of their calls in balance and harmony. The work of the Nine Doors is the mainstay of a grand system synthesizing the world of the scholarly runologist or historian of religion and that of the magical practitioner or skald.

The completion of the Ninth Door will be the manifestation of this synthesis.

Reading

During the course of this Door you will begin to decide what your master-work toward becoming a Fellow and eventually a Master in the Gild will be. There will be specialized readings for these studies. Some will be drawn from the works contained in the bibliography, while many more will come from outside that list. It is in this area that the Runer's developed sense of investigative prowess will be proven.

Daily Work

Unlike any of the previous Doors, there is no recommended time limit on the completion of the Ninth Door. Only you will be able to determine when the work is finally finished. Certain aspects of the Door are just continuations of previous work. However, the final synthesis of your work, both in some objective outer form and in the form of your inner metamorphosis, may already be complete, or it may be years away.

Road-Wending II
Runic Journeys through the Worlds

By now a set of symbolic keys have been provided for you at this stage of your development so that you can go on to explore the Rune-roads and Rune-streams on a new level.

In your previous work with the Yggdrasill model you have been looking at it from an objective point of view. You have seen the pattern from the outside and entered it to do your work from that angle. Now, however, you will work from the subjective viewpoint— from the inside.

To do this, imagine yourself in Midgard (where you truly are) with the intention of exploring as many of the worlds and realms throughout the Yggdrasill model of the world as you can. You will guide yourself along the road-ways leading from Midgard to the various other worlds and back again to Midgard. It will be noted that certain path-ways are easier to gain access to and travel along than others. The Yggdrasill pattern in Figure 9.1 shows a map of the "flow patterns" of the Tree. The road-ways in black flow most easily in a downward direction, those in gray flow most easily in an upward direction, while those in white flow in either direction with equal ease. The Runer will most often want to go in the path of least resistance— but sometimes you will find that you have to go against the flow— to swim up stream or go down a rough road.

The most difficult world to reach is Asgard, the least difficult are Jötunheimr, Vanaheimr, Svartálfheimr and Ljóssálfheimr— although none can be said to be easy.

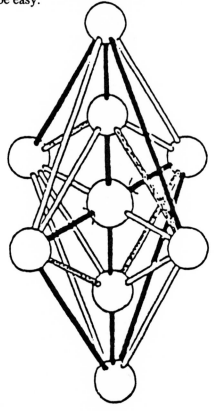

Figure 9.1: The Flow Patterns in Yggdrasill

As you enter into any path-way from the subjective point of view — from inside the model — let your imagination have full reign. As you enter through the door-way— see the landscape of the road-way. Imagine yourself to be on an actual journey— how will you go? Will you go on foot, on horseback, in a wagon? What or whom do you see on this journey? What does it mean to you? The results of each of these Journeys should be noted in your Galdor-Book, and used for future reference. If you had undertaken these kinds of exercises at an earlier point in your runic development, the results would certainly have been interesting but they would have probably been highly subjective and personal. Now that you have absorbed a good deal of the objective aspects of the runic tradition, your results can be expected to have a more objective quality.

Seið-Work II
Útiseta
(The Rite of Sitting Out)

From the last Door you learned how to begin to make contact with entities from other realms in a very direct way. The traditional rite of sitting out (ON *útiseta*) is a kind of seið-work in which the Runer will make contact with his or her own personal warden or fetch and gain on-going interaction with it.

The fetch (ON *fylgja*) has a variety of kinds. There are the *dýrfylgja* (animal fetch), *mannsfylgja* (personal fetch) and the *kynfylgja* (clanic fetch). Here we focus on the personal fetch. It is the repository of all "personal" action and power, both advantageous and disadvantageous. It or she is commonly known as a "following spirit"— but ironically it is usually seen to appear going before a person in the shape of a woman, animal, or a crescent shape) and is usually only visible to those with "second sight" or more generally to those who are about to die— the fey (ON *feigr*, OE *fæge*). The fetch is an aspect of the psychosomatic complex that may be reborn from generation to generation. (All this was more fully discussed in the introduction to the Other Door) Unfortunately, most persons remain totally unaware of its/her presence, and therefore take no steps to make contact it or her to gain the wisdom and power residing in the fetch.

A warning must be given here: The fetch is not an omnibenevolent being— contact with it may throw an individual self into a maelstrom of "bad luck." This all depends upon the faithfulness of that individual's past action. However, in the long run, contact with the fetch is always a positive act, no matte what the immediate results may be. The fetch usually imparts an abundance of "spiritual" gifts upon the individual who makes contact with her. The concept "fetch" is a rather generic one. This also may encompass more precise aspects of the concepts *dís*, *valkyrja*, *norn* (all feminine), and the masculine concept *álfr*. That is, only when this kind of entity is attached to a particular individual.

The working of sitting out is well illustrated in the "Helgakvíða Hjörvarðssonar" in the prose section before stanza 6 through the prose after stanza 9. There we read a reflection of *útiseta* in which the seeker goes and sits on a burial-mound or howe (ON *haugr*) in order to make contact with the "realm of the dead" (that is, realms other than Midgard). The seeker makes contact with his valkyrie, who gives him his true name, Helgi (the Hallowed One), a sword (symbol of power and contact with the "spiritual self") as a name-gift (ON *nafnfestr*) and her personal protection.

In theory there are several ways to contact the fetch, but in this instance it is through contact with the "realm of the dead" that communication is effected. It will be remembered that the fetch is consistently described as becoming visible to the fey (also think of the popular phenomenon of the life [= past actions] passing before the eyes of a dying man). Therefore, it is the task of the Runer to induce a trance-like state of false-death, under mental and physical conditions favorable for the manifestation of the fetch in the consciousness of the individual.

To do this several steps need to be followed:

(1) Familiarize yourself with the idea of the fetch as much as possible— know what you are looking for— ignorance of our true natures is the greatest barrier to knowledge.

(2) Meditate for some time (over the span of several days) on the concept, and what it means to you. In its undifferentiated state the fetch may be visualized as a crescent, or a sphere of light hovering in front of you. In these meditations, visualize the form of your individual fetch. Is it a geometrical shape, an animal form, or a contra-sexual form? Try to determine the name of the fetch if at all possible. Take note of any other helpful clues that might be useful to you when you perform the rite.

(3) When you feel prepared go on to the formulation and performance of the sitting out working.

Útiseta-Working

1. Dress: Wear whatever is comfortable and in clothes that have been dedicated to Rune-craft. The cloak and hood of the Runer are perhaps best.

2. Preparation: The Runer should prepare should prepare him or herself as well as the site on which the sitting out is to take place. Mental preparation includes a) ritual donning of the garments to be worn at the rite nine hours before the rite is to begin, b) maintaining of ritual

silence for the following nine hours, 3) hourly meditations on the purposes and goals of the rite. All of this should take place on or within sight of the stead of working. Concerning the stead-of-working itself: it should be outside, preferably on a hill-top or at a cross-roads (old country cross-roads, for example). In the case of the cross-roads; the work-stead should be in the north western quadrant. The site must be secure from intruders, and in an isolated place. The best time for a work of this kind is during the waxing or full moon. The Runer will need a vessel of mead, a drinking horn or cup, and the proper evocatory verses committed to memory.

3. Opening: Once the preceding conditions have been met, the rite may begin. At dusk, walk to the exact site of the ritual. Perform the proper hallowing working to clear the stead, and to make it ready for your working. Take up position in a comfortable sitting posture, with the mead and drinking horn nearby. Facing northward, meditate on your personal past and your family— let a feeling of love rise up in your heart for your clan, and for its most ancient branch in the days of the Elder Troth. After about 30 minutes, lapse into an inner silence— and hold a solemn vigil of a considerable time (2-3 hours, or more if necessary). The important function of the vigil is the general evocation of the numen— a feeling of "otherness" should begin to come upon you in a short while. At this time do not concentrate on the object of the rite, just allow the numinous feeling to grow— bask in the sensations of its power.

4. Call: At the right moment, recite the invocatory galdor. This should be composed by you, embodying as many of the specifics known about your fetch as possible. A hypothetical galdor could read:

> Fly southward   swan-white maid,
> through murk-wood wend thy way;
> thou my bride,   to me thy brother
> tell elder tales of bygone days
>   and of my deeds and doom.

5. Drinking: (the Full): Pour the mead from the vessel into the horn or cup. (Individual capacities for alcohol should determine how much mead may be consumed — do not drink yourself into a stupor — the purpose is the call to inspiration — not unconsciousness or hallucination.) Hold the horn out in front of you, elevated to the heavens and recite the toast (full) to your fetch. This should be a stanza of praise, honoring your fetch— and at the same time your clan. An example could be:

Fierce battle-maid   friend of Mardöll
   daughter of Dorruðr;
thy byrnie shines,   bright thy shield,
   weal is thy wyrd!

Drink half of the horn in one draught, and pour the rest onto the ground in front of you, then place the horn to your right side.

6. Song: Assume a comfortable, relaxed posture and begin to intone the song of final invocation (this may be done out loud, or silently, or in a combination of the two). An example song could be: "Þuriðr thunder forth!" chant this over and over, and begin to try to visualize the form of the fetch before you. (She has always been there.) You may have your eyes closed or open for this. Continue to chant the song, concentrating on the form of the fetch. This is where the preliminary meditations and visualizations will have helped. After some time of solid contact, lapse into a deep silence.

7. Binding: In a semi-trance state, attempt to communicate with the fetch. Ask her to reveal her name, her lineage, and to give you your Rune-name, and a gift of power or wisdom that goes with it. Also, form this point on, you will be deeply obligated to the fetch and her kin, the valkyries and dises. This communication may take any other directions as well.

8. Return: After the contact is complete and the "conversation" is ended, call her back into your sphere with the words: "Fetch fly back!" or something similar. She will return to an area just in front of your chest.

9. Closing: Close the ritual in a simple version of your normal procedure— and leave the site.

You may informally contact your fetch at any time after this. Within 24 hours you should perform a blessing in the name of your fetch, in which she will be worshiped as a true goddesss.

A simpler method, from the folk-tradition, of finding out what one's animal fetch is to put a knife in a white cloth and hold the bundle over your head. While doing this repeat the names of all the animals you know, and when you come to the name of the species of your fetch, the knife will drop out of the cloth.

The End of the Fellow's Path

If you have completed the work of the Nine Doors as outlined in this book, you will have become eligible, as far as the training component is concerned, to be named a Fellow in the Gild— but this can only come after you have chosen to join the Rune-Gild and make a life-time commitment to it. Otherwise Gilders will have to have completed the first four Doors of Midgard in order to be named a Fellow— or have undertaken an equivalent curriculum of magical study, and he or she must make contact with a Master of the Gild, so that a personal evaluation can take place.

Toward Becoming a Rune-Master
(The Rune-Master's Work)

Runic studies and Rune-work are not intended for everyone, as you have found out if you have worked your way to this point in the Nine Doors program. The Runes embody (are) our most sacred mysteries— reserved for study by the best of our number. You have begin to set out on this road-way. Now the course of work that you will be expected to complete in order to become a true Runemaster is not that difficult if you are literate and intelligent— which we assume you are if you have gotten this far!

To be considered for naming as a Master in the Gild, one needs to meet several qualifications. Two of the most important ones are the completion of a "Master-Work" in Runelore, and a personal examination of the candidate by at least two Masters of the Gild. At least one of these must be done face to face. No one can be named a Gild-Master who has not laid a physical Master-Work ("masterpiece") on the table.

The Master-Work of Lore

Instead of a "lesson" type approach in which many would probably be inclined to repeat back thoughts contained in a fairly limited set of text materials— we opted for a more comprehensive and flexible self-designed curriculum. The final result of this will be a tangible work of objective value.

The basic readings for this final process should already be known to you from the bibliography printed in this book. You should have already mastered the contents of most of the important works on that list as you worked your way through the curriculum of the Nine Doors.

After you have explored and worked with these readings, you may settle on a tentative topic for your work. This topic must be approved by the High Rede of the Gild— we are also available to offer you suggestions for topics once general areas of interest or competence have been established. Ultimately, you should submit a project proposal to be approved by the High Rede and the Steward of the Gild. This proposal should consist of a title, outline, and a short synopsis of what you have in mind.

As far as the nature of the topic is concerned, the material in the bibliography and other Gild materials indicate the wide variety of types to chose from. There is virtually no limit to what we can explore from the runic angle. Preferred topics can, of course, be classified within the fields of runology, theology, cosmology, or philosophy, but other areas are by no means excluded.

One practical matter the Gild can probably help you with, if necessary, is that of bibliography. Find books and other sources for your work. Some topics will, it is true, require vary few reference works, for example works of original synthetic thought. But others will require, or at least be greatly aided by, fairly extensive specialized reading.

The completed Master-Work should be typed (double spaced), and the text itself should be *at least* 5,000-7,000 words in length, but really publishable book-length manuscripts are preferred. The work should be accompanied by a complete bibliography and footnotes if it is the kind of work that would benefit from these features.

More extensive details on this work are available to Gilders in the *Gildisbók*.

A Master-Work is the sign that your knowledge has ripened to the extent that you can offer your fellows within the Gild an example of your thought. This will demonstrate for all to read that you have mastered the process of acquiring information and ideas from various sources, synthesizing them with your own experience and nature, and then re-expressing that synthesis to your fellows in a way that stimulates and informs them. This is the intellectual side of Odianism. As Wōden wins the Runes (the paradigmatic mysteries of the multiverse) absorbs them into his being, and finally speaks their secrets to his human allies, so too must we follow his example and so do the same within our great ring.

The Master-Work of the Self

In the final analysis a Master (or a Fellow for that matter) can only be known and Named through personal contact with the Masters of the Rune-Gild. Although some of this can be carried out through correspondence, the Gild is not a "mail order operation"— the true examinations and initiations must take place face to face. Ample opportunity to interact with Gild-Masters is offered through the World-Moots of the Rune-Gild which are held in various locations. Only through this direct person to person contact can the true self of the Runer be seen and recognized for what it is.

Appendix A
Tables of Basic Runelore

The most fundamental image of Runelore is the complete Fuþark divided into the three *ættir* (or airts) as shown in the figure below. Beyond this there is the basic historical and esoteric Runelore, which appears in the following tables.

ᚠ ᚢ ᚦ ᚨ ᚱ ᚲ ᚷ ᚹ

ᚺ ᚾ ᛁ ᛃ ᛇ ᛉ ᛈ ᛈ

ᛏ ᛒ ᛖ ᛗ ᛚ ᛜ ᛞ ᛟ

1 ᚠ   Proto-Germanic name: *fehu*: cattle; mobile property
       Gothic name: *faihu*: cattle, mobile property
       Old English name: *feoh*: cattle; money
       Old Norse name: *fé*: livestock; money, gold

LORE: Rune of wealth and expansive energy. Rune of new beginnings and the circulation of power.

2 ᚢ   Proto-Germanic name: *ūruz*: aurochs
       Gothic name: *urus*: aurochs (urus)
       Old English name: *ūr*: ox, bison
       Old Norse name: *úr*: drizzle, rain; slag

LORE: Rune of vital power and will. Rune of formation and organic structuring.

3 ᚦ   Proto-Germanic name: *þurisaz*: giant (thurs, strong one)
       Gothic name: *þiuþ*: the good one
       Old English name: *þorn*: thorn
       Old Norse name: *þurs*: giant

LORE: Rune of reactive and directed force— catalyst for change through resistance.

4 ᚨ   Proto-Germanic name: *ansuz*: ancestral sovereign god
       Gothic name: *ansus*: a runic god-name (divine ancestor)
       Old English name: *ōs*: a god; mouth
       Old Norse name: *áss*: a god; an estuary

LORE: Rune of ancestral sovereign power of the mind consciousness, inspiration, enthusiasm, and the power of the use of symbols for transformation of consciousness. Rune of Wōden.

5 ᚱ Proto-Germanic name: *raiðō*: a wagon; riding
    Gothic name: *raiþa*: wagon; ride
    Old English name: *rād*: riding; way
    Old Norse name: *reið*: riding; chariot; thunder clap

LORE: Rune of ordered change and progress. Rune of rationality and right order — which is a dynamic process — in the world.

6 ᚲ Proto-Germanic names: *kēnaz*: torch; or *kaunaz*: sore
    Gothic name: *kusma*: swelling
    Old English name: *cēn*: torch
    Old Norse name: *kaun*: sore, boil

LORE: Rune of creativity and of technical ability to shape things in the objective and subjective worlds. The Rune of art.

7 ᚷ Proto-Germanic name: *gebō*: gift; hospitality
    Gothic name: *giba*: gift
    Old English name: *gyfu*: gift; generosity
    Old Norse name: *gipt*: gift; wedding (not in younger row)

LORE: Rune of the gift— of exchange between two poles. The Rune of the sacrifice of self to self and self to one's fellows bringing honor to the self. Rune of hospitality and generosity.

8 ᚹ Proto-Germanic name: *wunjō*: joy
    Gothic name: *winja*: pasture
    Old English name: *wynn*: joy, pleasure
    Old Norse name: *vend*: (Rune-name) joy, hope (not in younger row)

LORE: Rune of pleasure and a feeling of harmony within the self and in the society in which you find yourself. The Rune of well-being.

9 ᚻ Proto-Germanic name: *hagalaz*: hail(-stone)
    Gothic name: *hagl*: hail
    Old English name: *hægl*: hail
    Old Norse name: *hagall*: hail (special Rune-name)

LORE: Rune of crisis and catastrophe. Condensation of powers into a seed-form from which further developments, positive or negative become possible.

10 ᚾ Proto-Germanic name: *nauþiz*: need, necessity, compulsion
Gothic name: *nauþs*: necessity, need
Old English name: *nȳd*: need, distress
Old Norse name: *nauð(r)*: distress, need, constraint

LORE: Rune of resistance— which can kindle a fire of higher will or which can constrain the self (or any process) and its development. Rune of the power of the ordeal in life.

11 ᛁ Proto-Germanic name: *īsa*: ice
Gothic name: *eis*: ice
Old English name: *ís*: ice
Old Norse name: *íss*: ice

LORE: Rune of constriction and coagulation. Rune of concentration of things in a static or frozen state.

12 ᚼ Proto-Germanic name: *jēra*: (good) year, harvest
Gothic name: *jer*: year
Old English name: *gēr*: year
Old Norse name: *ár*: year, good harvest

LORE: Rune of reward for, or reaction to, actions in a horizontal (naturally ordered) cyclical process. Rune of the results of actions.

13 ᛇ Proto-Germanic name: *īhwaz*: yew tree
Gothic name: *eihwas*: yew tree
Old English name: *eoh*: yew tree
Old Norse name: *ihwar*: yew (in runic inscriptions only)

LORE: Rune of the verticality of enlightenment. The axis of the spiritual or intellectual process of becoming. Axis of unity between the upper and nether worlds meeting in Midgard.

14 ᛈ Proto-Germanic name: *perþrō*: lot-cup
Gothic name: *pairþra*: dice-cup
Old English name: *peorð*: gaming piece (?)
Old Norse name: (not used in younger row)

LORE: Rune of the Nornic process of birth-life-death-rebirth. Rune of change and the evolutionary process.

15 Y Proto-Germanic names: *elhaz*: elk; or *algiz*: protection
Gothic name: *algis*: swan (?)
Old English name: *eolh*: elk
Old Norse name: *ihwar* —> *ýr*: yew, yew bow (in runic
inscriptions only)

LORE: Rune of the essential link or connection with the patterns of
divine or archetypal consciousness. Rune of the possible danger of
realizing this link when unprepared.

16 ? Proto-Germanic name: *sowilō*: sun
Gothic name: *saugil*: sun
Old English name: *sigil*: sun
Old Norse name: *sól*: sun

LORE: Rune of guidance from an outside source in the process of
making a journey or transformation of any kind. Rune of the light of
the inner sun, and its link with the outer sun— both of which are signs
of the goal of the process of Runework.

17 ↑ Proto-Germanic name: *tīwaz*: the god Tīw (ON Týr)
Gothic name: *teiws*: the god Tīw
Old English names: Tīw: the god Tīw; *tīr*: glory
Old Norse name: *týr*: the god Tīw (Týr)

LORE: Rune of balance and justice ruled from a higher rationality. The
Rune of sacrifice of the individual (self) for the well-being of the
whole (society).

18 ß Proto-Germanic name: *berkanō*: the birch goddess
Gothic name: *bairkan*: birch twig
Old English name: *beorc*: birch (tree)
Old Norse name: *bjarkan*: birch (special runic name)

LORE: Rune of the containment and release of energy leading to
continued growth and continual rebirth or renewal in all things. The
Rune of liberation and becoming.

19 M Proto-Germanic name: *ehwaz*: horse
Gothic name: *aihws*: stallion
Old English name: *eh*: war-horse
Old Norse name: *ior*: (not found in younger runic row)

LORE: Rune of harmonious teamwork and trust. Rune of pairs of entities working together for a common goal. Rune of the outside partner in this configuration.

20 ᛗ Proto-Germanic name: *mannaz*: human
    Gothic name: *manna*: human
    Old English name: *mann*: man, human
    Old Norse name: *maðr*: a man, human being

LORE: Rune of the divine structure of intelligence in the human soul or psyche. Rune of awareness, and the awareness of the horizons of human existence.

21 ᛚ Proto-Germanic names: *laguz*: water; *laukaz*: leek
    Gothic name: *lagus*: water
    Old English name: *lagu*: sea, water
    Old Norse name: *lögr*: sea, water

LORE: Rune of the context of becoming or evolutionary processes— which may be at times largely unconscious (re. *laguz*). Rune of the matrix of action. Rune of upward growth out of roots in the unconscious to unfoldment and blossoming in the light.

22 ᛜ Proto-Germanic name: *ingwaz*: the (Earth-)god Ing
    Gothic name: *engus* or *iggws*: the god Ing, a man
    Old English name: *ing*: the god Ing
    Old Norse name: Ing or Yngvi (name of Freyr)

LORE: Rune of isolation or separation in order to create a space or place where the process of transformation into higher states of being can occur. Rune of gestation and internal growth.

23 ᛞ Proto-Germanic name: *dagaz*: day
    Gothic name: *dags*: day
    Old English name: *dæg*: day
    Old Norse name: *dagr*: (not in younger row)

LORE: Rune of the final synthesis of consciousness— the ultimate enlightenment of mind.

24 ᛟ Proto-Germanic name: *ōþala*: ancestral property, estate
    Gothic name: *oþal*: property
    Old English name: *ēþel*: homeland, property
    Old Norse name: *oðal*: nature, inborn quality, property
     (not in younger row)

LORE: Rune of the homeland— the spiritual state of internal well-being, freedom and security in which development and growth can take place.

Summary of the Lore of the Elder Fuþark

Name	Sound	Shape	Meaning
fehu	f	ᚠ	CATTLE (wealth, dynamic power)
ňruz	u	ᚢ	AUROCHS (vital formative force)
þurisaz	þ	ᚦ	ÞURS (giant, breaker of resistance)
ansuz	a	ᚨ	GOD (Wōden, sovereign ancestral god)
raiðō	r	ᚱ	CHARIOT (vehicle on path of power)
kēnaz	k	ᚲ	TORCH (controlled energy)
gebō	g	ᚷ	GIFT (exchanged powers)
wunjō	w	ᚹ	JOY (harmony of like forces)
hagalaz	h	ᚻ	HAIL (destruction, seed form)
nauþiz	n	ᚾ	NEED (distress, self created fire)
īsa	i	ᛁ	ICE (contraction)
jēra	j [y]	ᛃ	YEAR (good harvest, orbits, cycles)
îhwaz	i	ᛇ	YEW (axis of heaven-earth-hel)
perþrō	p	ᛈ	LOTBOX (evolutionary force)
elhaz	-z	ᛉ	ELK (protective teaching force)
sowilō	s	ᛊ	SUN (sun-wheel, crystallized light)
tîwaz	t	ᛏ	TYR (sky-god, sovereign order)
berkanō	b	ᛒ	BIRCH(-GODDESS, container/releaser)
ehwaz	e	ᛗ	HORSE (trust, cooperation)
mannaz	m	ᛗ	HUMAN (psychic order of the gods)
laguz	l	ᛚ	WATER (life energy, organic growth)
ingwaz	ng	◊	ING (earth-god, gestation process)
dagaz	d	ᛞ	DAY (twilight/dawn paradox)
ōþala	o	ᛟ	ESTATE (ancestral spiritual power)

Appendix B
The Rites of the Rûna-Workshops

All Runers who are working with the Nine Doors are encouraged to set up runic study groups, officially called Rûna-Workshops when they are authorized by the Rune-Gild. (Write to the Gild for an application to register your Rûna-Workshop, which could eventually evolve into an Outer Hall of the Gild— which has its own special Hall-Workings.) The activities of the Rûna-Workshops should also include ritual work. Members of the Workshops may experiment with doing versions of their Daily Work together, or they may improvise other workings from authoritative runic sources.

Officially, there are three main group workings for members of the Workshops:

1) Opening the Workshop
2) Draught of Fellowship
3) Closing the Workshop

These three workings should be done at every Rûna-Workshop meeting. The discussions, talks, or other runic experiments should come after the Draught of Fellowship.

This format helps to ensure that the discussion of Runelore will be carried out in an atmosphere of sacrality and that the members of the Workshop will have a sense of fellowship (*wunjō*) among themselves.

Opening the Workshop

The Workshop steward (the permanent leader of the group of one so designated for this particular meeting) opens the meeting by rapping three times on wood with his or her gand, saying:

I now call this meeting of the Rûna-Workshop open. I call upon you to lift your minds toward the mightiest Rune— as we seek after the Runes lying within and without. May we rown our words aright!

All then perform the Gild version of the Hammer-signing rite (see Door II) together.

The Draught of Fellowship

The steward then loads a container of liquid (this could be a bottle of mead, ale, wine, or fruit juice) by tracing the sign of *wunjō* (w) over it and saying:

By the might of *wunjō* we are all come together in good fellowship to rown of the Runes and of the wonders of Wōden!
Wassail!

All repeat: Wassail!

The steward then pours out some of the loaded liquid for each of the participants. Once all have full glasses, they raise them on high and all call together: Wassail! and drink some or all of the liquid in their glasses.

This concludes the Draught of Fellowship and sets the mood for any discussions, lessons, or work to come.

Closing the Workshop

The steward brings the Workshop meeting to a close by asking:

Is our work here at an end?

If there is general agreement, the steward closes the Workshop by saying:

Our work is at an end for now— but ever are we on the road to the Runes.

The steward then raps three times with the gand and says:

Wassail!

All repeat: Wassail!

Appendix C

Introductory Information
>>The Outer Hall of the Rune-Gild<<

(Valid After 2005ce)

Runes are the mysteries that underlie all of the worlds— that which lies *hidden* in, and gives power to, all things. These Runes pull those who seek them ever onward and upward. Knowledge of them and the quest for their mastery, both within the self and throughout the worlds, is the Path of Odin. This quest leads to transformation— in the Self and in the Worlds.

As a practical matter, the Odian Path has, until recently, been obstructed by a general lack of available information on a refined and authentic level. The Rune-Gild has undertaken to remedy this lamentable situation. But beyond this goal, our intention is to provide a gateway into the practical application of runic principles. It is imperative that a number of individuals be initiated into the intellectual and working aspects of runology. The soul of our folk has little chance of survival — much less of being as great as it is destined to become — if it is not armed with the Secrets of the Self. These secrets are the Runes.

Because knowledge of the Runes has languished under suppression in the distant past, and under ill-conceived superficial studies in the more recent past, it is now necessary that seekers along the true Rune-roads gain deep and sound intellectual knowledge along with more practical work in Runecraft. Knowledge and Work must always go hand in hand.

History of the Gild

The Rune-Gild was founded in 1980ev as the first authentic rebirth of the elder Runic tradition to be available to the new Gilders in about a millennium. Over the ensuing years, the Gild has grown and changed its form as new information and impulses entered into its knowledge base— and as its leadership became more initiated. However, our aim has remained true and steadfast— to see the elder Runemasters again make their wisdom known and felt in the world of their descendants. This is a great task, for those interested in the heritage of the Germanic or Gothic peoples— and this includes all those who live in countries where a Germanic language (f.ex. English) predominates — it may indeed be the greatest task that lies before us. For without the deep level spiritual heritage to guide us we will surely be lost in a morass of cultural confusion. The Runes stand ready, the Masters know their duty, but each Gilder must work for his or her own initiation. The doors of the Gild-Hall now stand open— enter with heart, enter with mind — and learn again the ways of the Runemasters.

With the publication of *Futhark: A Handbook of Rune Magic*, *Runelore: A Handbook of Esoteric Runology*, and *Runecaster's Handbook: At the Well of Wyrd* the gates were opened. The time has now come to have those of you who will, enter the first doors of a gradual approach to Rune-Work and Rune-craft. In the Rune-Gild you will be introduced to a graded series of exercises known as the *Nine Doors of Midgard*. In these exercises you will learn various techniques of Rune-Work: more explicitly of Rune-thinking (meditation/ contemplation), Rune-casting (divination), galdor (incantational or verbal magic), making of Rune-tines (talismans) and other forms of Rune-craft (operative magic) and most important of all Rune-Work (self-transformational activity), as well as many other techniques that were only touched on in a cursory fashion in *Futhark* and *Runecaster's Handbook*. The first three books by Edred were the beginning— the Rune-Gild itself is a road which is itself a goal.

The curriculum of the Gild is based on the oldest and most traditional runology of the Erulians. From this traditional base— which all profane approaches to the Runes recently published lack — Gild-members will be guided to levels of knowledge completely unavailable through other avenues.

The rationale of the existence of the Gild is this: In olden times there was a Rune-Gild — an intertribal network of those initiated into Rune-Knowledge — this network (or gild) was unique. It was a feature of the established culture in ancient times. The Rune-Gild is in fact a remanifestation of this network. The absolute *proof* of this is that the leadership of the Gild is qualified in the established intellectual world: its leader in a Ph.D. in Germanic studies with a dissertation entitled *Runes and Magic*, its members are well-published authorities on the subjects of the Runes and the Germanic tradition. The Gild is not a theater for occultizoid nincompoops or starry-eyed elf-viewers. It is the core of a serious cultural movement. The Rune-Gild has all the hallmarks of the true and authentic remanifestation of the Gild of old. It is a traditional school dependent on personal contact now as it was in ancient times, and it will remain dependent on this contact forever. This is the way it was, the way it is, and the way it shall be forever.

Structure of the Rune-Gild

In the Outer Hall of the Gild there are three levels, or "degrees," of initiation. These are based on the most ancient steps of learning any skill known in the elder age— that of apprentice, journeyman, and master. In the terminology of the Gild, however, these are reflected in the names or titles Learner, Fellow, and Master.

The Gild is divided into Inner and Outer Halls. The Outer Hall of the Gild is made up of the Learners and Fellows of the Gild, guided by the Gild-Masters. If there is a Hall-Leader in your area who is running a Gild-Hall, there will also most likely be Outer Hall Workings and gatherings which you could attend. Also, members are encouraged to set up Rûna-Workshops ("runic study groups") in geographical areas where no Hall exists. Many Gilders in the Outer Hall will be working alone, or in Rûna-Workshops. It can not be said too often that the Gild does not deal in "mail-order occultism."

The Inner Hall is made up of those who have completed the *Nine Doors of Midgard* curriculum, or its equivalent, and who have been *personally* inducted by a Gild-Master as a Fellow of the Gild.

The Outer Hall the Gild is not overly formal in its organization— it is rather like an extended magical study group. The practical advantages to actual membership in the Outer Hall are the extensive personal contacts that can be made, information on all the latest developments in the world of Rune-Work, and most importantly the inner keys to making the Hall-Workings true *magical bonds* between yourself and the Gild-Halls (both Inner and Outer) around the world.

A word might be mentioned on the Gild-Masters and Drightens. They are a distinguished group of individuals each with their own area of expertise, each with their own unique gifts to offer the Gild. The Yrmin-Drighten, Edred, is the author of a number of books, including the major "textbooks" of Rune-Gild Work. He also holds a Ph.D. in Germanic Studies from a major university.

Goals of the Gild

Among the most important goals of the Gild are the continued development of traditional and transformational Runelore and the dissemination of that system to those who are inspired by the quest for the Runes. We continue to institute Rûna-Workshops around the world. In addition to this, there is an ever expanding network of Outer Gild-Halls open to members who are personally invited by a local Hall-Leader to join a Gild-Hall.

It can not be overemphasized that the main work of the Gild is centered in each individual, and its main aim is the self-transformation of each Gilder according to the ancient Odian principles. For it is only from this basis of transformed individuals that the new Gild can be reborn in the full essence of the elder Gild of the Erulians.

For such transformations to occur there come key moments in the individual development of each Runer when *personal* contact with a true Runemaster is Needed. The Rune-path may *begin* in solitude, and may end there, but in the middle there comes a time to interact with those who bear the Flame and who can show it to you.

To this end the foundation of the first permanent Hall of the Gild — the Yrmin-Hall — was laid in late 1993 and it was fully erected in the early part of 1994. It is situated on 30 acres of land near Austin, Texas. From 1997 to 2005 the Gild held annual Gild-Moots in urban areas around the world— after that time the Gild became more decentralized and its activities became more widespread. At present the Gild is very well-developed in various parts of the USA and in England, where its activities are guided by the Drighten, Ian Read and the members of the Eormensûl Hall. The whole history of the Gild up to the year 2005 is outlined in the book: *History of the Rune-Gild* vol. III, available form Rûna-Raven Press.

The Work of the Gild can be summed up in the Seed-Word ***Rûna*** — "The Mystery," especially as extended and articulated through the stave: *Reyn til Rûna*— "Seek toward the Mysteries!" *Rûna* is the Hidden in the World, and the Sense of the Hidden lying within the depths of the Self. This eternal Quest is the essence of Rune-Work— and its fulfillment is the highest goal of the Gild.

The Doors of Valhalla stand wide open. It is now your Work to step forth through the Doors of Midgard to face the challenges of a new way of being that awaits you within. The Gild stands ready to help you in this Work— as no other organization in the world today can do. We welcome those who now wish to join us in the Runic quest!

Entry into the Gild

To become an Associate of the Rune-Gild, and begin your possible road toward becoming an actual initiated member of the Gild you must first register with the Gild as an Associate. This can be done on the website: **www.runaraven.com** or by sending $50.00 in the USA, $70.00 overseas with a basic letter of introduction. All prospective Associates are strongly urged to visit the website: **www.runegild.org** to find a wealth of up-to-date information about how the Gild works.

The initial toll is a one-time fee. Unless and until you are invited to become a Learner in the Gild, you will not be asked for any further fees or tolls. For this initial fee you will receive a package of materials through which you can become more familiar with the inner workings of the Gild. These include the seminal guide to the Gild: *The Gildisbók*. This book takes you beyond the curriculum of the Nine Doors and guides you more deeply in the fulfillment of the work of the Nine Doors.

Previously individuals had to gain sponsorship from a Gild Master in order to gain access to certain materials. This is no longer the case. Now prospective members can access certain key concepts, work with them, and, if the flame is ignited in them and their work takes off, they can seek Apprenticeship with one of the Masters of the Gild. In a manner of speaking we have relaxed access to certain ideas, but at the same time made the Gild a much more exclusive and personalized operation. The true work of the Gild takes place both within the individual soul and in the process of the various interpersonal relationships which develop between and among Learners, Fellows and Masters.

The Rune-Gild
P.O. Box 557
Smithville, Texas 78957

Or Visit our websites at:

www.runaraven.com
and
www.runegild.org

The Rune-Gild website will also inform you about how to make contact with the Gild in various parts of the world outside the USA.

Reyn til Rûna!

Readings

1. Inner Working Techniques

There are only a few reliable books on traditional esoteric Runecraft and Rune-Work. However, the following bibliography may give some hints as to the kind of texts the Runer unfamiliar with "occult teachings" might read in order to get some idea of the scope and character of the work involved. Most of these books are only good from a *practical* viewpoint— as their *theoretical* backgrounds are generally non-Odian and therefore not to be taken seriously by the Runer. Members of the Gild are encouraged to explore various quality literatures, and to develop a critical mind...

Further commentaries on these texts are found in the *Gildisbók* of the Rune-Gild.

Butler, W.E. *Magic: Its Ritual Power, and Purpose.* London: Aquarian, 1952.

Butler, W.E. *The Magician: His Training and Work.* North Hollywood: Wilshire, 1959.

Buzan, Tony. *Use Both Sides of Your Brain.* New York: Dutton, 1974.

De Ropp, Robert S. *The Master Game.* New York: Dell, 1968.

Denning, Melita and Phillips, Osborne. *Creative Visualization.* St. Paul, MN: Llewellyn, 1989, 2nd ed.

Harner, Michael. *The Way of the Shaman.* New York: Harper and Row, 1980.

Knight, Gareth. *Occult Exercises and Practices.* New York: Weiser, 1976.

LaVey, Anton Szandor [=Howard Stanton Levey]. *The Satanic Bible.* New York: Avon, 1969.

Lysebeth, Andre van. *Pranayama: the Yoga of Breathing.* London: Unwin, 1979.

Ophiel [Edward Peach]. *The Art and Practice of Getting Material Things Through Creative Visualization.* St. Paul, MN: Peach Publishing, 1970.

Ouspensky, Peter D. *The Psychology of Man's Possible Evolution.* New York: Knopf, 1969.

Sadu, Mouni. *Concentration: A Guide to Mental Mastery.* North Hollywood, CA: Wilshire, 1959.

Samuels, Mike and Nancy Samuels. *Seeing with the Mind's Eye: The History, Techniques and Uses of Visualization.* New York: Random House, 1975.

Steddinger, Inga. *Wiccan Sex-Magic.* Smithville: Rúna-Raven, 1999.

Wood, Ernest. *Concentration: An Approach to Meditation.* Wheaton, IL: Theosophical Publishing House, 1967.

2. Runology: Exoteric and Esoteric

In the exoteric, or scholarly, field this category is not very well represented in English. But in the esoteric, or magical, area it must also be said that we have begun a quality revival of traditional Rune-lore that is unrivaled in any language. So the future does look brighter than in the recent past. There have been many books on Rune magic published since the early 1980s. Most of them are misleading to any one on the true Rune-quest. Runology, esoteric or exoteric, is a complex business – and like most complex things of any real value – it is best left to experts. The books on this list are the *only* ones that can be recommended by the Gild on any level. All others are best left unbought and unread. If any Gilder has a question about a book not on the list, or wishes to bring one we might not know about to our attention, please write to the Yrmin-Hall.

Elliott, Ralph. *Runes: An Introduction.* Manchester: Manchester University Press, 1959.

Flowers, Stephen E. *The Galdrabók: An Icelandic Grimoire.* York Beach, ME: Weiser, 1989.

Flowers, Stephen E. *Runes and Magic: Magical Formulaic Elements in the Older Runic Tradition.* New York: Lang, 1986. (op)

——————, ed. *The Rune-Poems.* Smithville: Rûna-Raven, 2002.

Kummer, Siegfried Adolf. *Rune-Magic.* (tr./ ed. Edred Thorsson) Austin: Rúna-Raven, 1993.

List, Guido von. *The Secret of the Runes.* (tr./ed. Stephen E. Flowers) Rochester, VT: Destiny, 1988.

Osborn, Marijane, and Stella Longland. *Rune Games.* London: Routledge and Kegan Paul, 1982.

Page, R.I. *Introduction to English Runes.* London: Methuen, 1973.

Page, R.I. *Runes.* Berkeley: University of California Press, 1987.

Thorsson, Edred. *Futhark: A Handbook of Rune Magic.* York Beach, ME: Weiser, 1984.

——————. *Runelore: A Handbook of Esoteric Runology.* York Beach, ME: Weiser, 1987.

——————. *Runecaster's Handbook.* [Formerly titled *At the Well of Wyrd*] York Beach, ME: Weiser, [1988].

——————. *Rune-Might: Secret Practices of the German Rune Magicians.* St. Paul, MN: Llewellyn, 1989.

——————. *Green Rúna: The Runemaster's Notebook.* (= the Shorter Works of Edred Thorsson: Vol. I) Smithville: Rúna-Raven, 1993.

——————. *Northern Magic.* St. Paul, MN: Llewellyn, 1993.

——————. *Rune-Song: A Practical Guide to Galdor-Work.* Austin, Texas: Rúna-Raven, 1993.

3. Germanic Religious History

In order to gain a well rounded picture of the context into which the Runes fit, it is important to be as familiar as possible with the religious consciousness of the ancient Germanic peoples. The more familiar the modern Runer is with the "mind-set" of the ancient Runers, the firmer his or her foundation for the future will be.

Byock, Jesse L., tr. *The Saga of the Volsungs*. Berkeley, CA: University of California Press, 1990.

Chisholm, James A. *Grove and Gallows*. Smithville: Rûna-Raven, 2002.

Dumézil, Georges. *Gods of the Ancient Northmen*. ed., tr. E. Haugen, et al. Berkeley: University of California Press, 1973.

Ellis (Davidson), Hilda R. *The Road to Hel*. Cambridge: University of Cambridge Press, 1943.

Ellis Davidson, Hilda R. *Gods and Myths of Northern Europe*. Harmondsworth: Penguin, 1964.

Ellis Davidson, Hilda R. *Myths and Symbols in Pagan Europe*. Syracuse, NY: Syracuse University Press, 1988.

Ellis Davidson, Hilda R. *The Lost Beliefs of Northern Europe*. London: Routledge, 1993.

Flowers, Stephen E. "Toward an Archaic Germanic Psychology," *Journal of Indo-European Studies* 11:1-2 (1983), pp. 117-138.

———————————— and James A. Chisholm. *A Source Book of Seiδ: the Corpus of Old Icelandic Texts Dealing with Seiδ and Related Words*. Smithville: Rûna-Raven, 2002.

Grimm, Jacob. *Teutonic Mythology*. tr. J.S. Stallybrass. New York: Dover, 1966. 4 vols. (first published 1835).

Hollander, Lee M. tr. and ed. *The Poetic Edda*. Austin, Texas: University of Texas Press, 1962.

Neckel, Gustav and Hans Kuhn, eds. *Edda: Die Lieder des Codex Regius nebst verwandten Denkmälern*. Heidelberg: Winter, 1962, 2 vols., 3rd ed.

Russell, James C. *The Germanization of Early Medieval Christianity*. Oxford: Oxford University Press, 1994.

Simek, Rudolf. *Dictionary of Northern Mythology*. tr. A. Hall. Woodbridge: Brewer, 1993.

Simpson, Jacqueline., ed. and tr. *Icelandic Folktales and Legends*. Berkeley: University of California Press, 1972.

Simpson, Jacqueline, ed. and tr. *The Penguin Book of Scandinavian Folktales*. London: Penguin, 1994.

Simpson, Jacqueline, ed. and tr. *Legends of Icelandic Magicians*. Ipswich: D.S. Brewer, 1975.

Sturluson, Snorri. *Edda*. tr. Anthony Faulkes. Rutland, VT: Charles Tuttle, 1987.

(Sturluson, Snorri). *Egil's Saga*. tr. H. Pálsson and P. Edwards. Harmondsworth: Penguin, 1976.

Tacitus, Cornelius. *The Agricola and the Germania*. tr. H. Mattingly. Harmondsworth: Penguin, 1948.

Turville-Petre, E.O.G. *Myth and Religion of the North*. New York: Hold Rinehart & Winston, 1964.

4. 20th Century German Occultism (and "Nazi Occultism")

Of enduring fascination to many on the Germanic path is the history of the abortive revival of Germanic culture and religion at the beginning of this century in Germany. This revival ended with the National Socialist regime in Germany, although it too incorporated those elements of the revival which suited its purposes. It is our task today to study dispassionately that era in order to extract that which was noble from that which was ignoble– and to make use of the noble aspects. This field is full of crank books– some of which are interesting to read. We suggest here the "classics" in the field.

Flowers, Stephen E. and Michael Moynihan. *The Secret King: Karl Maria Wiligut— Himmler's Lord of the Runes*. Smithville/Waterbury Center: Rûna-Raven/Dominion, 2001.

Goodrick-Clarke, Nicholas. *The Occult Roots of Nazism: The Ariosophists of Austria and Germany 1890-1935*. Wellingborough, UK: Aquarian, 1985.

Pauwels, Louis and Jacques Bergier. *The Morning of the Magicians*. New York: Avon, 1968.

Ravenscroft, Trevor. *The Spear of Destiny*. New York: Putnam, 1973.

Webb, James. *The Occult Establishment*. La Salle, IL: Open Court, 1976.

5. General Philosophical Works

Besides gaining a thorough foundation in specifically Germanic magic, myth and religion, the Runer should become familiar with more general studies in these fields. These you will be able to apply directly to your Runic studies as you absorb their contents.

Flowers, Stephen E. *Rúnarmál I*. Smithville, Texas: Rûna-Raven, 1996.

——————————. *Blue Rûna: Edred's Shorter Works, Vl III (1988-1994)*. Smithville: Rûna-Raven, 2001.

——————————. "The Idea of Integral Culture: A Model for a Revolt Against the Modern World." *Tyr– Myth-Culture-Tradition* 1 (2002), pp. 9-21.

Jacobi, Jolande. *The Psychology of C.G. Jung*. New Haven: Yale University Press, 1973 [1942].

Jung, Carl. *The Archetypes and the Collective Unconscious*. (=Bollingen Series 20, vol. 9 pt. 1 of the Collected Works) tr. R.F.C. Hull. Princeton: Princeton University Press, 1959.

6. General Mythology and Religious History

Besides understanding the particularly Germanic mythological viewpoint, it is also important that the Runer gain a deep level understanding of the wider Indo-European vista.

Benveniste, Emile. *Indo-European Language and Society*. tr. E. Palmer. Coral Gables, FL: University of Miami Press, 1973.

Campbell, Joseph. *The Hero with a Thousand Faces*. (= Bollingen Series 17) Princeton: Princeton University Press, 1949.

Eliade, Mircea. *A History of Religious Ideas*. tr. W. Trask. Chicago: University of Chicago Press, 1978-1985, 3 vols.

Eliade, Mircea. *The Myth of the Eternal Return or Cosmos and History*. (=Bollingen Series 46) tr. W. Trask. Princeton: Princeton University Press, 1971 [1954].

Eliade, Mircea. *Rites and Symbols of Initiation*. tr. W. Trask. New York: Harper and Row, 1958. (Also published as *Birth and Rebirth*.)

Eliade, Mircea. *Shamanism: Archaic Techniques of Ecstasy*. (=Bollingen Series 76) tr. W. Trask. Princeton: Princeton University Press, 1964.

Eliade, Mircea. *Yoga: Immortality and Freedom*. (=Bollingen Series 56) tr. W. Trask. Princeton: Princeton University Press, 1958.

Flowers, Stephen E. *Studia Germanica I*. Smithville: Rûna-Raven, 2000.

Gennep, Arnold van. *The Rites of Passage*. trs. M.B. Vizdom and G.L. Caffee. Chicago: University of Chicago Press, 1960.

Littleton, C. Scott. *The New Comparative Mythology: An Anthropological Assessment of the Theories of Georges Dumézil*. Berkeley: University of California Press, 1973, 2nd ed.

Mallory, J. P. *In Search of the Indo-Europeans: Language, Archaeology and Myth*. London: Thames & Hudson, 1989.

Otto, Rudolf. *The Idea of the Holy*. tr. J.W. Harvey. Oxford: Oxford University Press, 1958.

7. General Historical Context

Besides esoteric and mythic/religious history, we must keep in mind the political and socio-economic aspects of the past– in order to keep things in proper perspective.

Davidson, H.R. Ellis. *Pagan Scandinavia*. New York: Praeger, 1967.

Flowers, Stephen E., ed. *Ibn Fadlan's Travel Report as it Concerns the Scandinavian Rús*. Smithville: Rûna-Raven, 1998.

Jones, Gwen. *A History of the Vikings*. Oxford: Oxford University Press, 1968. (Also a second revised edition.)

8. Alternate Religions in Contemporary Perspective

Although the Rune-Gild is an independent entity, its existence is to some extent tied into certain larger movements, both social and magical. It is very wise for the Runer to have a handle on these movements and the place of the Germanic Renaissance within it.

Adler, Margot. *Drawing Down the Moon*. New York: Viking, 1979. (2nd ed. 1986.)

Chisholm, James Allen. *True Hearth: A Guide to True Householding*. Austin: Rúna-Raven, 1993.

Flowers, Stephen E. "Revival of Germanic Religion in Contemporary Anglo-American Culture." *Mankind Quarterly* 21:3 (Spring, 1981), 279-294.

Miller, David L. *The New Polytheism: Rebirth of the Gods and Goddesses*. New York: Harper and Row, 1974. (Also a more recent paperback edition.)

Thorsson, Edred. *A Book of Troth*. Smithville: Rûna-Raven, 2003, 2nd ed.

——————. *Witchdom of the True*. Smithville: Rûna-Raven, 1999.

9. Cosmology

One area of lore in which the Germanic tradition is quite distinguished in the realm of cosmology. Unfortunately, this is again another area in which there is very little representative literature. *Runelore* begins to fill in much of the gap (so-to-speak!), but the field is awaiting a classic work.

Bauschatz, Paul C. *The Well and the Tree*. Amherst: University of Massachusetts Press, 1982.

Zoller, Robert. *Skaldic Number-Lore*. Smithville: Rûna-Raven, 1999.

——————. *Towards a Germanic Esoteric Astronomy*. Austin: The Rune-Gild, 1986. (op)

To obtain Rûna-Raven titles, visit the website at:
www.runaraven.com

CPSIA information can be obtained at www.ICGtesting.com
Printed in the USA
BVOW081953220812

298513BV00003B/105/P